Care Proceedings

Robert Dingwall
and *John Eekelaar*

Care Proceedings

A Practical Guide for Social Workers,
Health Visitors and Others

Basil Blackwell · Oxford

© Robert Dingwall and John Eekelaar 1982

First published 1982
Basil Blackwell Publisher Limited
108 Cowley Road, Oxford OX4 1JF, England

British Library Cataloguing in Publication Data

Dingwall, Robert
    Care proceedings: a practical guide for social workers, health visitors and others.
    1. Children – Legal status, laws, etc. – England
    I. Title II. Eekelaar, John
    344.204'32795   KD3305

ISBN 0-631-12756-9
ISBN 0-631-12757-7 Pbk

Phototypesetting by Oxford Publishing Services, Oxford
Printed and bound in Great Britain at
The Camelot Press Ltd, Southampton

Contents

Preface

This book was written as a consequence of a research project conducted by the authors, together with Mrs Topsy Murray, at the SSRC Centre for Socio-Legal Studies, Oxford, with funds from the Social Science Research Council and the Department of Health and Social Security. That project investigated the relations between health, social work and legal agencies in identifying and managing cases of child abuse and neglect. A report has been submitted to the funding bodies and the study will be the subject of a book, *Protecting Children, Controlling Parents: State Intervention in Family Life*, to be published by Basil Blackwell, Oxford, towards the end of 1982. In the present book, however, we have tried to use our experience from that research to respond to a need recognized by many people in the participating agencies, namely a practical guide to the legal issues which come up in child protection work. Reflecting the multidisciplinary nature of this area, our intended readership includes not only social workers but also doctors, whether in hospital, community or primary care, health visitors and other community nurses, teachers and probation officers. We hope that it will be as useful for students in these occupations as for experienced practitioners.

What we have tried to do is to describe the legal provisions and procedures which are relevant to children in need of care or protection as they stand in England and Wales at 30 September 1981. Throughout, however, we have linked our description to the practical questions which confront people working in this area: what procedures are best suited to which kinds of case? what are the implications of using one statute rather than another? what kind of evidence is needed and admissible? how can we determine where a child's interests lie? When the law is silent or uncertain, we have tried to indicate what might constitute good practice. Moreover, in an area where the law may be applied flexibly, we have tried to show how the letter of statutes and regulations is, typically, interpreted in a spirit of common sense. Above all, we have tried to explain why certain procedures take the form that they do, bringing out some of the deeper issues which set the constraints under which each agency plays its part in the task of child protection. Unless these are recognized, people can easily become frustrated and blame the difficulties of establishing satisfactory working relationships on 'personality clashes' rather than the inherently different roles allocated to each organization or occupation.

This book does not apply either to Scotland or to Northern Ireland. Many of the basic issues are common throughout the home countries but the legal and institutional systems are so different that separate books would really be needed if each were to be covered adequately.

Robert Dingwall
John Eekelaar

Acknowledgements

The research on which this book is in some measure based was carried out in collaboration with Topsy Murray. We wish to record our debt to her part in that study and thank her for allowing us to draw on her experience in administering social services cases for a local authority legal department. This book has been much improved by her critical reading of the early drafts. Considerable assistance has also been rendered by Pam Watson, whose careful scrutiny has contributed greatly to the intelligibility and coherence of the final text. We should also like to thank Malcolm Colledge, Liz Morgan and Judith Rayner for reading the drafts from their various backgrounds in law, community nursing and social work. The successive typescripts have been prepared by Rosemary Stallan. We are grateful for her deep reservoir of patience and good humour in the face of our revisions and amendments.

Chapter 1

Identifying Children in Need of Protection

We were concerned at the general impression given by witnesses regarding their knowledge of the law. We heard of one social worker who had been in post for a very short time and admitted to having no real knowledge of child care law. Quite senior officers had no knowledge of wardship as a method of protecting children.

Paul Steven Brown Inquiry   1980

[East Sussex] took the decision not to oppose revocation of the care order in 1971 upon insufficient evidence and upon a misapprehension of the evidence.

Maria Colwell Inquiry   1974

For the best part of the last decade, public inquiries into the conduct of child protection agencies have pointed to the importance of a clear understanding of child care laws as an essential part of good professional practice. Those same inquiries, however, have repeatedly documented the failings of staff, at all levels and from all agencies, in this respect. Despite the improvements that have taken place in both basic and in-service education, many people involved in child care still become very hesitant and anxious when confronted with the legal issues that inevitably come up in the course of their work. To be fair, many of these issues are comparatively uncommon: fewer than three children in every thousand come into care in any one year. While social workers will be involved in all these cases, and have some opportunity to build up their experience, few members of any other occupation ever encounter legal questions often enough to develop any real expertise and confidence. Just as importantly, however, many people have felt little motivation to improve their legal knowledge. For some of them, the very idea is contrary to the whole spirit of their work. 'Caring' is, quite wrongly, thought to be incompatible with legal understanding. We think that this attitude is mistaken. A degree of legal knowledge is important for workers in all agencies, not because of the remote threat from some public inquiry but because most British health and welfare services are created or regulated by Acts of Parliament.

The parliamentary system may be an imperfect instrument of democracy. Nevertheless, it is the means which we have in this country for expressing a formal collective view on what we are prepared to consider acceptable standards of conduct and on the ways in which we hope to encourage such conduct or to discourage alternatives. The various Acts which lay certain duties upon child protection agencies and grant them certain powers to support the execution of those duties represent a set of directions about what we as a society consider to be the reasonable goals of professional practice and appropriate means of achieving them. Given the complexity of the social and moral issues which arise in child protection, there are inconsistencies, ambiguities and anomalies in the legislation which allow scope for the exercise of professional discretion. Such discretion can, however, only operate within the limits set through the law.

Although law lies at the heart of professional practice, the people involved may find it difficult to understand, especially as that understanding involves some familiarity with the expressions and concepts of an alien discipline. This is not to say that all social workers, health visitors or doctors need an advanced training in law, any more than legal practitioners in this area need similar training in medicine, nursing or social work. What is required is an informed appreciation of the positive contribution that other disciplines may have to make, such that specialist advice can be obtained at the right time and used appropriately.

Professional practice in child care will fall short of the highest standards unless it is carried out in reasonable awareness of its proper legal context. At the very least a 'laicized' version of the relevant laws must be absorbed into the basic strategies of case management. In assimilating that law, agency staff will be taking due account of the popular consensus which provides both financial and moral support for public services. Child care law is one of the means, however imperfect, by which citizens guide those who act on their behalf.

Finding the Victims

Children who are in need of care or protection do not display that need like some sort of label round their necks. Between a child's suffering and the intervention which may relieve it there is a gap which is filled by acts of interpretation within a variety of agencies. Somebody has to see a child, to determine that that child is in need of care or protection and persuade others of the correctness of that interpretation. The first step in considering child protection, then, is to ask how children are found, by whom, as a result of what sort of inquiries. This is particularly important in the British system because, while most of the significant powers are held by social services, social workers are seldom the first people actually to make an identification in any particular case. Moreover, in this country, the agencies which do identify are under no general legal obligation to refer cases for possible intervention. In order to discuss this screening process, we have made a rough division of agencies into those which do most of their work in public places and those which go into the home to survey family life.

This division is related to a very basic principle in societies like ours. What we do in public is open to anybody's gaze: what we do in private is our own affair. Unfortunately, those private matters may have public consequences. In this specific instance, the quality of social reproduction – the nature of children's upbringing and their preparation for the responsibilities of adult life – is something which has far-reaching implications for our political, economic and moral order. It is this general concern which can justify the invasion of privacy, but the very concept of 'private life' itself sets limits to the intervention that is possible.

Family Surveillance

Those agencies whose staff regularly go into people's homes have a particular advantage in identifying children's needs for care or protection. They can simultaneously assess both the child's actual condition and his or her immediate social, physical or moral environment. Such access is particularly important for small children, who are much less visible, socially, than their older brothers or sisters. As children grow up, they spend more and more time in public settings – attending school, playing in the street, drifting round shopping centres or sitting in cafes.

While some services, like education welfare or probation, follow children into their homes once they have been picked out in public places, the only agency which systematically reviews the child population is the health service or, more precisely, its community and primary care sectors. This activity derives from the duty of the Secretary of State for Social Services, under section 1 of the National Health Service Act 1977, to promote 'a comprehensive health service designed to secure improvement in the physical and mental health of the people . . . and in the prevention, diagnosis and treatment of illness'. Section 3(1)(d) expands on this, requiring the Secretary of State to provide 'such . . . facilities for the care of expectant or nursing mothers and young children as he considers are appropriate as part of the health service'.

The National Health Service is in the process of being re-organized as this text is being written. Nevertheless, this is not likely to make a great deal of difference to those parts of the structure which we are describing here, although some job titles may change.

Community health staff are employees of District Health Authorities (DHAs). Typically, they have separate medical and nursing divisions reporting through their own managerial lines to the District Medical and Nursing Officers (DMO and DNO). Prior to reorganization, community medical officers would be responsible, although often only in a rather loose sense, to a Specialist in Community Medicine (Child Health). Community nurses – health visitors, district nurses, school nurses and, in some areas, community midwives – formed part of a more clearly bureaucratic structure reporting through a line of Nursing Officers (NOs) and Senior Nursing Officers (SNOs) to a Divisional Nursing Officer (DivNO). Most authorities also had a specialist policy and development adviser, an Area Nurse (Child Health). It is not yet possible to say how far these posts will be retained and how the management structure will be organized below District level.

Primary care services are provided by general practitioners (GPs) who are independent contractors rather than employees. GPs enter into an agreement with the National Health Service to provide primary medical care for people registered with their practices. In return, they are paid a basic annual fee for each registered patient, weighted by age, and additional fees for undertaking certain specific tasks like family planning or ante-natal care. Historically, their focus has been on the treatment of ill-health, either by their own prescriptions or by onward referral to specialists based in hospital. Recently, however, there have been moves towards a more preventive orientation. As part of this, many GPs have taken over the provision of routine child health clinic services from the community medical divisions' staff. Most community nurses are now attached to general practices, but they remain the managerial responsibility of the community nursing division. Community nurses work *with* rather than *for* general practitioners.

By and large, community medical officers and GPs see children in clinics or surgeries, rather than at home. The numbers of children involved are quite substantial: every year about three quarters of all children under fifteen will visit a GP for some illness, averaging four to five consultations each; and about eighty per cent of all children under one year are seen at clinic sessions, although that falls off quite sharply to less than a third of two- to five-year-olds. Nevertheless, even these opportunities for identifying children's needs are limited by comparison with those available to health visitors. In any one year, health visitors see over seventy per cent of all children under five, including almost every new baby, in their own homes.

Health visitors are registered nurses with recognized obstetric training who have completed a one-year certificate course (HV Cert). This course combines academic instruction, in psychology, sociology, social policy, social epidemiology and health visiting principles, with supervised practical experience. Although there is a small, and growing, number of men in the occupation, most health visitors are women. Their caseloads tend to be high. The 1972 DHSS recommendation of one health visitor to 3,000 population is rarely approached, and ratios go as high as one to 10,000 and more in some metropolitan districts. This translates into caseloads of anywhere between 250 and 1,000 individuals, most of whom will be children under five. All births are routinely notified and visited, although the visiting schedule is a matter for the health visitor's discretion. It is difficult to generalize about these home visits but, typically, they last about twenty minutes. In the course of this time, the health visitor attempts to make some assessment of the home environment and each child's physical, emotional, cognitive and social development, and to respond to any problems raised by the child's caretaker (almost invariably the mother).

One of the commonest misconceptions held by other agencies is that health visitors have a legal right of entry to people's homes. They do not: their access to any household is entirely dependent on the goodwill of the residents. This is an important constraint and relates to the general notion of privacy which we raised earlier. As such, the constraint applies equally to other health workers and, indeed, to most agencies. When access to a household is by invitation, it is difficult for any child protection worker to act in an openly investigative manner or to offer unsolicited advice. In the case of health visitors, the problem is confounded by their limited access to resources which clients might want and which could act as an inducement for them to cooperate.

Health visitors are in a uniquely favourable position for identifying the needs of young children. Their combination of knowledge about both physical and social factors in growth and development bridges the gap between doctors and social workers, who tend to specialize in one or the other. They have a vast experience of looking at normal children in ordinary homes, which helps them to recognize signs or symptoms that might be overlooked by people with less representative experience. Moreover, their characteristic work pattern of unannounced home visiting allows any special interest in a child to be concealed. If there is concern about a child's nutrition, for instance, a health visitor can 'accidentally' call at mealtimes. This can be very useful in cases where anxiety about a child's welfare has not crystallized into a clear basis of evidence which might justify the firm identification of a need for care or protection. Wherever there is concern about a child under five, it is advisable to consult the relevant health visitor at an early stage. Indeed, if the child who is causing concern is over five but has siblings below that age, it is still likely to be worth involving the family's health visitor for what she can offer on the history and current state of the household.

Other community nurses may occasionally become involved in child protection. The most important of these are community midwives. Health authorities vary greatly in the way in which the care of mothers and babies is divided between midwives and health visitors. In general, however, midwives carry out home visiting of new mothers from their confinement, or hospital discharge, until the tenth day after birth. Antenatal visiting forms part of their duties in some areas and they are also empowered to follow cases for up to twenty-eight days after birth. This clearly gives them an opportunity to monitor a child's home circumstances and the quality of care he or she is receiving. On the other hand, this contact is probably too short to be of great value except in alerting other agencies to possible problems. Its most obvious uses are likely to be in identifying the need for various sorts of voluntary intervention such as assistance with housing or care for other children during confinement or illness in pregnancy. Where a pregnant woman is under seventeen and unmarried, the question may arise as to whether she should come into care in her own interests, which might also allow for more effective protection of her baby.

District nurses also have a minor role in child protection. Some of their work is with sick children where concern might develop about their parents' ability to provide continuing care. They are also occasionally used to monitor children in a household where they are ostensibly nursing an old person. A clinical reason for frequent visiting may be more acceptable to the family than a high level of health visitor surveillance.

Although both health visitors and community midwives have received specialized training for their work with children, this is not necessarily the case for either community medical officers or general practitioners. Neither group has, up till now, been required to have any substantial training in child health. For general practitioners, this is changing as the new system of vocational training is phased in, but it will still be some years before this can make an appreciable impact. Even so, neither group will be able to match the degree of social understanding and the experience of normal children possessed by community nurses. This is a very important point for people in other agencies. There is an inevitable tendency to accept medical opinions without questioning their basis. At the same time, community nurse reports are often discounted, despite their possibly greater validity.

Staff in other agencies also need to bear in mind the low level of integration in child health services. All of the occupations involved have strong and jealously guarded traditions of autonomous practice. This is as true of community health services, with their apparently bureaucratic structures, as it is of general practitioners under their independent contracts. This means, for instance, that people should not assume that if they give information to a GP it will also go to his attached nurses, or vice versa. The same applies to communication within community health services and the flow of messages between fieldworkers and managers.

In the case of general practitioners, some of the obstacles to the sharing of information are related to legal anxieties. A doctor is, in general, open to being sued for breach of confidence if he passes on information about a patient to a third party without that patient's consent. Since 1968, the Medical Defence Union has advised its members that passing on details of child abuse, without the consent of the child or his or her parents, to local authority social services or the NSPCC would be legally defensible but is not an obligation. This opinion should be strengthened by the 1977 decision of the House of Lords, in the case of *D* v. *NSPCC*, which held that, in the interests of public policy, the NSPCC should not be compelled to disclose the identity of its informants. Local authority social services would almost certainly be covered by the same principle. On the other hand, this may not be very helpful where we are considering suspicions rather than firm indications. Moreover, since most of the doctor's dealings with a child are through the intervention of a parent, the child's interests can easily be overlooked. Where a child is suffering as a result of mental disorder in a parent, for example, the prospect of further damage to the adult may override consideration of the, separate, case for the child's removal. If legal proceedings were to result, the Guardianship of Minors Act 1971, section 1, lays down that the courts 'shall regard the welfare of the minor as the first and paramount consideration'. By extension, the same principle should be applied in assessing cases which could result in proceedings. This, of course, may be easier said than done in the face of the interpersonal and community pressures that a parent can bring to bear on a practitioner.

Most other home visiting services, as we remarked earlier, depend upon following up referrals from agencies which are engaged in surveying children in public places. It will therefore be more convenient to discuss them as extensions of such surveillance.

Public Surveillance

Once again, the health services have a substantial role here, through school health, accident and paediatric services. With these older children, however, we must now add the educational and criminal justice systems to the list of surveillance agencies.

Theoretically, the school health service extends the general screening of children's health and development from the age of five until school leaving. Where disorders of growth or behaviour are identified, children should be referred for more specialized intervention, referrals which may bring them into the care and protection system. The school health service, however, is widely recognized to be in a rather unsatisfactory state. It relies heavily on part-time staff, both doctors and nurses, whose knowledge and commitment are less than complete and whose efforts are often poorly organized and ill coordinated. Some areas have been trying to improve matters and there are, of course, many individuals with a considerable depth of interest and concern. Nevertheless, much will depend upon these unpredictable local variations as to the contribution which this service can make on any particular occasion.

Accident and Emergency Departments see large numbers of children – between a quarter and a third of all patients are under fifteen. However, the work is unpopular with doctors and the departments are particularly dependent on overseas-trained staff and on those who are required to obtain A and E experience as part of their specialist training in surgery. Because of differences in cultural background, the former may have great difficulty in assessing British-born children. The latter are looking towards careers in general or orthopaedic surgery rather than paediatrics. In consequence, accident departments tend to have a narrowly clinical focus, responding to the presenting injuries rather than making the broad appraisal of a child's general condition which is the first step in considering the possibility of a need for care or protection. Paediatric accident departments staffed by doctors with appropriate knowledge of, and interest in, child health are found only in a few urban areas. An important, but often unrecognized, contribution could be made by nurses or other locally recruited staff, like receptionists or ambulance crews, in making rather wider assessments of a child's condition in relation to his or her social environment.

Unfortunately, there is often no institutional channel through which this can be communicated, especially if the medical staff are insensitive to its possible relevance.

Most hospital specialties can impinge on children's welfare in their treatment plans for adult patients. The admission of an adult to hospital may mean a child coming, temporarily or permanently, into local authority care. As we have already pointed out, these implications can easily be overlooked in concern for the adult involved. On occasion, the child's interest is at stake more directly. This is perhaps most obviously the case in obstetrics, where decisions about the clinical management of childbirth may have implications for the mother's perception of her baby and their ability to form a satisfactory relationship with each other. Wherever children are permitted to visit, ward staff have an opportunity to observe parent/child interaction. There are a few occasions on which this could be significant. For instance, where a woman has been admitted with injuries suspected, but not acknowledged, as resulting from a beating at the hands of a husband or cohabitee, observation of her children might be important in deciding whether there is some threat to their health or welfare. On children's wards, of course, the patients have been admitted because they are in need of health care. If there are welfare issues, these are already likely to have been identified, although ward nurses may be able to collect further data. One case which has arisen was where a child, who had come into hospital with unexplained gastric and neurological symptoms, failed to respond to treatment. When observed, the child's mother was seen to administer tablets to her and it was revealed that the symptoms resulted from deliberate poisoning.

The medical specialty most involved with children is, of course, paediatrics. Its central focus is the health of children, their illnesses and disorders of growth or development. Along with the parallel specialty of child psychiatry, its contribution is likely to be crucial in any case which involves the physical or mental state of a child. Where such a case has arisen, the relevant doctors should be brought in at an early stage to make a comprehensive and authoritative examination of the child if there is any possibility, however slight, of legal action. If possible, this examination should be carried out by a consultant, or at least a registrar, rather than a house officer. Legal intervention may prove unnecessary, but this should ensure that the decision for or against proceeding is taken with adequate clinical evidence available.

People from other agencies often find hospital medical staff easier to deal with than GPs. In part this reflects the more hierarchical organization. Once some policy is agreed with the consultant, then he is likely to ensure that it is followed by his junior staff. There are frustrations. Initial contacts may be with relatively inexperienced doctors who have difficulty in establishing exactly what is expected of them. It is important, then, that the referrer gives as much background information as possible and is able to point to the implications of the clinical findings and the standards they may have to meet as evidence. Access can also be a problem if the child's GP is obstructive. Sometimes it is possible to make referrals through community medical staff. A few paediatricians will accept 'under the counter' referrals from health visitors and social workers. One possibility is to use a referral to Child Guidance, which can lead to a child psychiatrist and thence to a paediatrician. In an emergency, of course, an injured or sick child may be taken directly to an accident department.

After the age of five all children should be in school. Indeed, if they are not then this in itself is a possible ground for deciding that a child is in need of care or protection. On the other hand, one must recognize how elastic the attendance standards are in many local education authorities. Quite frequently, inquiries only begin when a child has been absent from school more than fifty per cent of the time or six weeks continuously. A great deal of schooling can be lost before there is any serious attempt to find out the cause, and it is a common complaint from magistrates that they are asked to make care orders on children who have almost reached the school-leaving age. Other agency staff often assume that teachers can be relied on routinely to monitor the physical state of children in their charge. If abuse has been suspected, for instance, reliance may be placed upon the child being seen stripped for physical education. Teachers, on the other hand, do not necessarily seem to consider this an appropriate part of their duties. It also appears that the children who are identified and referred to education welfare or child guidance tend to be those who cause trouble in class. We do know, however, that at least some children react to long-term abuse or neglect by becoming very quiet and withdrawn, behaviour which may pass unnoticed.

Finally, we must mention police and probation services. Both have a dual role here: involvement with delinquent children, and with children who have other needs for care or protection. The first is relatively unproblematic in the sense that both agencies have an accepted place in dealing with juveniles who are committing or have committed offences. In recent years, the water has been somewhat muddied by the debate as to whether juvenile criminality is, in essence, a symptom of an underlying need for care or protection or whether it is to be dealt with in the same way as adult criminality. There is, however, little disagreement that somebody ought to be identifying children who are committing offences.

The protection role is less clear-cut. The police have traditionally acted as a temporary repository for lost or abandoned children, who may well go on to local authority care, at least in the short term, on a voluntary basis. More controversial situations do exist though. Women's groups have been strongly critical of police responses to domestic violence and their preference for a peacekeeping rather than a law enforcement type of approach. The police, it is said, would rather negotiate a settlement than prosecute an abusive spouse or cohabitee. This complaint is not an issue for the present book, except inasmuch as it seems plausible to suppose that children's interests may also be overlooked in the course of such peacekeeping efforts. Are they at risk of physical harm, if not intentionally, then at least by getting in the way of violence between adults? Alternatively, what psychological effect is this violence having on their development? It could be argued that these cases should routinely be referred to social services, whether or not enforcement action is taken.

Debate has also arisen over the degree to which other agencies should involve the police in cases where they have identified possible criminal offences. Naturally the police insist that if they are told of a case they must, as with any report of a possible crime, carry out an investigation and decide whether a prosecution would be appropriate. Other agencies, however, tend to feel that any police involvement is likely to be inconsistent with therapeutic objectives. This is an area where much depends on the level of trust and understanding which has been established locally. It is fair to say that the police have shown themselves increasingly sensititive to some of the criticisms which have been made of their investigative methods and prosecution policies. The police are under no duty – statutory or otherwise – to prosecute in every case where they are satisfied that sufficient evidence exists. On the other hand there is a whole set of criminal offences relating to assaults on children or negligence in their care which presumably reflect some sort of popular sentiment about the desirability of prosecution in certain cases. It is for the police in their use of discretion to balance this sentiment against the desire of other agencies to avoid criminal proceedings.

It must be conceded that, on the other hand, the police do have their own problems in persuading some of their junior officers to adopt less flat-footed approaches in their inquiries and in their dealings with other agencies. There do seem to have been genuine difficulties here following the break-up of the Women's Sections after the Sex Discrimination Act 1975 and the dissipation of the expertise and contacts which their officers had built up. The sort of understandings about the use of discretion which can be negotiated between senior officers of the police and other agencies are often difficult to implement within the force. Nevertheless, where other agencies have been persuaded to adopt a less hostile attitude to the police, the latter's response has often been notably constructive.

In their role as family welfare officers for divorce proceedings, probation officers should be routinely considering whether the children of a household should be placed in the care of a local authority. Where they are dealing with adult offenders, however, other issues arise. Like GPs, probation officers may have difficulty in disentangling the interests of adult clients and their children. Nevertheless, probation staff do have access to people's homes and, as such, have an opportunity to monitor standards of child care. When we get into these marginal aspects of work roles, though, as with district or hospital nurses, one can question how far there is a specifically professional duty here, or whether we are really talking about something which any citizen might be doing if they had the access.

Citizen Surveillance

We have concentrated, so far, on agencies which have the identification of children in need of care or protection as part of their professional duties. We should not, however, overlook the part which all citizens may have to play in this area. Particularly where a need arises in the home, it is likely to be most visible to friends, relatives and neighbours, any of whom could be involved in referring it for possible intervention. Yet this is a somewhat hazardous business. Obviously in such a situation there are powerful interpersonal pressures against referral. More-over, an observer may be uncertain of the standards to apply. In an area where most children are ill-kempt and poorly controlled, how is any particular family to stand out? Both of these features may also be used by the recipient of the referral to discount its significance. Anyone who makes such a report may be sus-pected of having a doubtful motive, or being hypersensitive to aspects of a family which would pass unnoticed in another context. Looking over a number of reports from child abuse inquiries, it does seem that hard-pressed agency staff are only too ready to pass over citizen referrals on such grounds.

In this chapter, we have drawn attention to the relevance of legal knowledge as an element of good professional practice in all child protection agencies. It is an important link in their chain of accountability to the public which sustains them. We have stressed that child protection can only result from the

identification of a case by some observer, who must then persuade others of the correctness of his or her judgement. The
agencies – health, education and criminal justice – which carry
out most initial identifications were then discussed in the light
of their access to information and knowledge about children
which might serve as a basis for their judgements. Different
combinations were seen to shape their interests and attention in
various ways.

Chapter 2

Intervention Agencies and Liaison Systems

A social worker has the full statutory powers behind him
. . . This power gives his visits and oversight of the care of
the child considerable significance, which a worker from
another agency can never have.

Maria Mehmedagi Inquiry   1981

Once a child has been identified as possibly in need of care or
protection, it will almost always be necessary to involve the
social services department of the relevant local authority. It is
these departments which control access to most of the legal and
institutional resources to support intervention, whether voluntary or compulsory. They do not, however, do much of the
initial identification. Relatively few child care cases actually
present themselves as such. Social workers more commonly
find they are dealing with adult problems – finance, housing
and the like – which may have implications for children. As we
have seen, though, people dealing with adult clients can have
difficulty in detaching themselves from the offered history and
in appraising children's circumstances as a separate issue. In
some respects, the NSPCC is in a similar position. The Society
shares the legal powers available to local authorities but depends
on others' referrals as a starting point for intervention. We shall,
therefore, also discuss its contribution in this chapter. Finally,
we shall consider the inter-agency arrangements – case conferences, at-risk registers and Area Review Committees – which

attempt to coordinate the activities of the organizations and occupations described in these first two chapters.

Social Services Departments

Social services departments are the executive arm of the social services committees which local authorities are required to establish under the provisions of the Local Authority Social Services Act 1970. As such they are, among other things, responsible for discharging the duties laid upon local authorities in respect of children living in their area. These include a general duty to make available 'such advice, guidance and assistance as may promote the welfare of children' and specific duties to receive children into care in certain circumstances, to investigate reports of children possibly in need of care and to bring children before the court in care proceedings, where appropriate. We shall examine these in detail when we discuss the legislative framework of child care in chapters 3 and 4.

The internal organization of social services departments varies more than the rather standardized pattern we have described for health authorities. There are three basic systems – divisional, large area, and divisional plus small area. In a divisional system, the local government area is broken up into a small number of large units, each of which centres on a main office responsible for both staff advice and line management. Typically, the headquarters staff is quite small. Most social workers are based at the divisional office and any sub-offices are used solely for calling in or, possibly, for small groups of staff under a local supervisor. In a large area system, the territorial units are rather smaller and staff functions are reserved to headquarters. Area Directors are usually responsible only for fieldwork personnel, with residential and domiciliary services coming under centrally-based line managers. The divisional plus small area system is a hybrid form which combines the devolution of policy formation and specialist resources of the divisional system with the greater local managerial scope of the area pattern.

Whichever arrangement is adopted, however, the most important thing for outsiders to recognize is that they are dealing with a local government bureaucracy. The notion of 'bureaucracy' has been rather disparaged in recent years. Much of this criticism misses the point. As a form of organization, bureaucracy emerged with modern states as the 'great chain of command' from rulers to citizens. With the spread of representative democracy, it became an instrument for the administration of those rules which citizens themselves had drafted to regulate their own society. One may criticize the practical imperfections of British politics by the standards of democratic theory, but these are more to do with the failings of representative government than the principles themselves. Something like a bureaucracy is an inevitable consequence of the sort of collectively provided services that we enjoy in a welfare state, making a link between those who are paying for services and those who are consuming them.

What this means, in practice, is that social services departments are organized in a fashion which is designed to reflect their accountability to elected representatives. This may be undercut by the inertia of electors or councillors, or by the unionization or professional aspirations of social workers, but it is nonetheless a basic working principle. Social work practice in local government, then, places considerable weight on the defensibility of its decision-making. This comes through in a number of ways. The two most important here are record-keeping and supervision. All social work decisions are elaborately documented and held on file for possible review. Thus it can be a matter of some significance whether a child is already known to the department by means of a file, and whether that file relates only to the child or deals with the whole family and various adult problems. Moreover, if a referral is made in writing, it will have to be filed and, since a record of contact has been created, some action will have to be documented, even if only a letter of acknowledgement. Telephone contacts have a much more ephemeral existence and cannot force the organization to respond with anything like the same effect. This attention to record-keeping is related to the close supervision of fieldworkers, with the object of ensuring that their practice conforms to departmental policy, that it does not incur financial or other obligations and that it does not exceed the department's legal powers or duties. Responsibility is constantly being transmitted upwards. Basic-grade social workers have relatively little discretion compared with GPs or even health visitors.

It is important to understand some of these factors in order to appreciate how social services handle reports of children in possible need of care or protection. There are two common complaints against them: of precipitate action and of undue delay. These may seem merely to suggest that social workers are in a situation where they cannot succeed, but both can be accounted for by features of departmental organization. GPs, for instance, sometimes complain that, having notified social services of a child about whom they are concerned but with whom they wish to deal themselves, the department has immediately initiated its own inquiries. What this complaint misses is that the department is under a statutory duty to make such inquiries unless it can be satisfied they are unnecessary. This places the onus on the referrer to give as full an account of the cause for concern and his or her intended action as is possible. That acount will, of course, have to be in writing. Even then, its adequacy is a matter for the judgement of the social services rather than the referrer. The second complaint can also be related to the demands of public accountability. Other than in a few well defined emergency situations, referrals to social services must go through a vetting and allocation process. To the referrer, of course, all referrals are urgent, but the department must ration its time and resources by looking at referrals in competition with one another. This is a problem which GPs in particular are seldom faced with, in the absence of effective cash limits on their practice costs. Once again, the force of referral is greatly enhanced if it is in writing and can, to some degree, speak for itself rather than through the mediation of a duty officer.

Social workers themselves are a very heterogeneous group. Many of the senior staff qualified before the advent of generic training and have specialized backgrounds in child care, mental welfare, almoning and the like. More recent entrants have come via both graduate and non-graduate routes. The former are again divided between those who have done accredited under-graduate degrees and those who have obtained postgraduate qualifications. So while the basic licence, the Certificate of Qualification in Social Work (CQSW), is the same, its substantive content varies considerably. Few departments come close to having all their social worker posts filled by qualified staff. The service has also gone through much more comprehensive re-organization than any other agency, and the first period of stability in over a decade, since the mid-1970s, has been one of increasing financial constraint. Inevitably there has been a great deal of confusion, debate and turmoil over the basic nature of the occupation's mandate. This lack of a positive identity has hindered relations with other agencies and the public, under-cutting the potential constituency of support in straitened financial circumstances, which have themselves complicated the search for a more adequately defined role.

Nevertheless, in the area of child protection, social workers control virtually all the key resources – money, substitute care placements, domiciliary support workers and access to the courts if legal sanctions are necessary. Effective intervention, in most cases, requires social service involvement. Obviously, the earlier this involvement occurs and the fuller the information on which it is based, the more chance it has of being useful.

The National Society for the Prevention of Cruelty to Children

Although the NSPCC's role as a private social police is something of an anachronism, it is still a body which enjoys considerable public respect and support. In 1979, for instance, over £2 million was raised in voluntary contributions and the Society also received rather more than £1 million from legacies. There were just over six thousand referrals from the general public and more than three thousand from official sources. Almost five thousand referrals came from parents themselves and another fifteen hundred from other relatives. The NSPCC still enjoys a unique power to initiate care proceedings, the only voluntary body to have this status. Again looking at 1979, the society brought 204 Juvenile Court cases and five private prosecutions of parents or caretakers.

The actual basis of the Society's activities, however, has been shifting away from the investigative role based on a national network of inspectors. In many respects this is seen as duplicating local authority efforts and one gets the impression that if a referral is found to have any substance it is quite likely to be passed on to social services for further action, with the inspector acting as a cut-out to preserve the anonymity of the original informant. The Society has increasingly concentrated on developing itself as a source of specialist knowledge and advice, complementing public-sector services with experimental and demonstration projects of various kinds and the creation of training schemes and resource centres.

The practical role of the NSPCC in any particular locality depends on the presence or absence of specialized activities and the basis of understanding with local social services. In some areas, the NSPCC is very much involved, maintaining child abuse registers, offering intensive casework and providing specialized investigative facilities. Against this, other parts of the country are dealing only with a thinly spread inspectorate, where one individual may be covering two or three counties.

Tying the System Together

It will already be apparent that the management of children in need of care or protection can be an extremely complex organizational problem, even before we discuss the involvement of lawyers and magistrates. A variety of workers with widely differing social and intellectual backgrounds and embedded in quite different sorts of agency structures must, somehow or other, communicate information and coordinate action. This has been, and is, an endemic source of trouble. Most areas have responded by attempting to develop some sort of inter-agency liaison system. Once again, the details vary greatly but certain features tend to be common. These include the existence of an Area Review Committee, the operation of an at-risk register and the use of local case conferences.

Area Review Committees (ARCs) stand at the apex of the system. They have been set up since 1974, following guidance issued in a series of circulars by the DHSS. Their membership is drawn from senior levels of the agencies we have described, generally chief officers or their deputies, although a few field-worker representatives may be included. As a body, a full ARC will probably only meet two or three times a year, but there are likely to be various subcommittees which come together more frequently. The ARC attempts to coordinate policy formation in the constituent agencies. It often organizes interdisciplinary training sessions and is also likely to oversee the local child abuse register, whichever agency actually keeps it. Generally, the ARC also issues an inter-agency procedure handbook which attempts to set out each agency's responsibilities and approach for the benefit of its own staff and those liaising with them. If the ARC is to be a workable body, however, certain major difficulties must be overcome. Since it lacks any statutory basis, it is entirely dependent on constituent agencies for its resources, which they, in turn, may have no authority to provide. More importantly, the lack of statutory powers poses a considerable enforcement problem. How can member agencies be sure that each will follow the agreed guidelines? The difficulty arises from the distinct objectives and duties of each agency, which means that each must reserve the right to disregard collectively agreed decisions in the light of its own responsibilities. ARCs vary considerably in the degree to which this is seen as a real possibility, or as an *ultimate* right, so that departures from agreed policies will normally lead to internal disciplinary actions. The closer a committee approaches the latter attitude, the more effective its work appears to be.

More tightly unified ARCs seem commonly to develop systems for the active monitoring of fieldwork practices. These tend to be based on panels drawn from the core agencies – community medicine and nursing, social services, police, NSPCC – but usually have one or two other members, depending on local circumstances and interests. Panels may operate largely on a paper basis, receiving and reviewing reports from case conferences at a local level. Alternatively, some areas use them as a kind of permanent case conference with local staff attending to present and discuss particular cases.

One of the most important functions of the Area Review Committee is its oversight of the local at-risk register. These registers, which go under various titles, are consolidated lists of children in the area who are formally considered to be at risk of abuse or neglect. In principle, any worker for a recognized agency can telephone a central number to ask whether a child is known. This facility is particularly important for emergency or out-of-hours services where the history implied by registration may be a crucial element in the interpretation of suspicious but inconclusive evidence from other sources. Registers vary considerably in the amount of information which they contain and the criteria for inclusion, although DHSS circulars have tried to encourage some uniformity. These general issues are the concern of the ARC. Specific decisions on registration almost invariably require the consent of a case conference at a local level and may be subject to ratification by the ARC or one of its subcommittees. In many ways, the registration procedure is more important than the register itself. The detailed local consultation which it provokes tends to make the central register irrelevant, since the first-line managers who would be involved in any suspicious emergency have the case brought to their attention. When questions arise, the fact of registration is already known without the need to consult the register. Particularly in non-metropolitan areas, many authorities have found the register to be surprisingly little used. Where it can be important in the present financial climate is in securing social service support – nursery places, day care, home help, etc. – which would not otherwise be available. This may provide an incentive for local areas to 'over-register' and apparently inflate the numbers of children thought to be at risk.

We have already introduced the term 'case conference'. These are local level meetings of interested agencies to exchange information on particular cases and coordinate future actions.

Again, there is a great deal of local variation in their authority. Some areas treat them as occasions for collective decision-making while others see them as essentially consultative. It does seem that they are more likely to operate effectively on the former basis, but there are difficult constitutional issues for those involved. Perhaps the greatest problem is that whereas the resources committed are likely to be those of the social services, they will probably be in a minority at any particular meeting. This applies even if the only purpose of the conference is to consider the possibility of adding a child's name to the local at-risk register. Anything which obliges social services to open a case and places constraints on its eventual closure adds to the demands on fieldwork time which is just as much a perceived cost as legal action or a care placement. How far can people who are not employed by the department, and hence are not answerable in the same way for their actions, impose such a commitment?

The case conference will also nominate an individual to act as 'key worker'. This person is usually someone who is already involved in the case and who takes on a coordinating role in relation to other workers. In effect, the key worker provides a day-to-day extension of the case conference's liaison role, checking that its decisions are indeed being translated into practice. As such, of course, this individual experiences the same problems of power and authority that we have already described for case conferences and ARCs. The key worker will generally be a social worker, since social services departments control most of the relevant legal and institutional resources. Exceptionally, however, it may be appropriate for another worker, possibly a health visitor or a general practitioner, to take on this task. The sort of situation we would envisage would be a sparsely-settled rural area where the greater decentraliz-ation of primary health care, compared with social services, may make it easier for a health worker to monitor a family and respond in an emergency. In an inner-city area we think it is probably inappropriate for health workers to assume this role simply to relieve social services. The dangers of this come through very clearly in the report of the inquiry into the death of

Maria Mehmedagi, where a health visitor became a key worker because of a strike by local social workers. Her own work suffered and the social services department was unable to give her adequate support. If anybody other than a social worker becomes the key worker on a case, it seems advisable to ensure that there is a clear understanding that, for this case, that person will have full access to social service resources as if they were a member of the department's staff. Moreover, the key worker should discuss the case with the local area director or an officer of similar standing at least as regularly as would an equivalently-experienced social worker – not less than once every ten to fourteen days.

In almost all areas, this committee network tends to be focused quite sharply on child abuse and neglect. It should be seen as an inevitable development from the public attention which has been directed to these topics over the last decade. These are not, however, the only reasons why children may need care or protection. The comparative underdevelopment of similar liaison schemes for other problems, say early warning of truancy or delinquency, may lead us to question whether, on the one hand, children with other needs are receiving an inferior, fragmented, service, or on the other whether services for child abuse and neglect have been over-elaborated and are now top-heavy with liaison systems that divert resources from other activities.

If intervention is required to protect a child's interests it will almost inevitably be necessary to involve the relevant local authority social services department. In doing this, workers in other agencies need to appreciate the constraints of a local government bureaucracy, organized as it is to facilitate accountability rather than swift executive action. The NSPCC has similar legal powers but fewer resources and is not, in any case, publicly accountable for its actions. The agency system is held together by various liaison arrangements formulated in high-level Area Review Committees and implemented through at-risk registers and local case conferences.

Chapter 3

The Legal Options

> . . . there is another major question that has troubled us,
> namely why the twins were discharged from care . . . We
> were not given any really satisfactory answer on this point
> as there was no long term plan which could have made the
> discharge consistent with the children's welfare, as the
> 1948 Act requires.
>
> *Carly Taylor Inquiry   1980*

There are three basic legal ways in which the state may become
involved in the care or protection of children. Although most of
these provisions relate to the activities of social services departments, an understanding of them is important for all agencies,
both in terms of recognizing the limitations of social workers'
powers and, more crucially, in identifying those cases which
should be brought to the departments' attention. Numerically,
the most important route is by voluntary reception under the
Child Care Act 1980. The most contentious is probably by
means of care proceedings under the Children and Young
Persons Act 1969. This Act also allows for children to come into
care as the result of committing an offence dealt with by criminal proceedings. Small numbers of cases arise in a variety of
family proceedings, of which the most significant are divorce
and wardship.

Although this book is largely concerned with care proceedings, it is not possible to discuss these in isolation from other
provisions. In many cases, the way in which a child comes into
care results from a choice, recognized or otherwise, between
legally permissible actions. Before discussing the 1969 Act

then, we shall summarize the other options which may be available. As with all the descriptions of legal provisions in this book, of course, our general account cannot be a substitute for specialized advice in the light of the actual facts of any particular case. What is important is that child protection workers should be able to recognize when such advice would be helpful and to use it in an informed fashion.

Acts of Parliament

Most people in child protection work will seldom need to look up the original statutes under which they work. Since the structure of our discussion in this chapter and the next takes the form of a commentary on particular provisions within these Acts, however, it may be helpful to describe briefly how a statute is typically laid out.

Acts of Parliament begin with what is, in effect, a list of contents, under the title *Arrangement of Sections*. Major pieces of legislation are generally split into a number of Parts. The Child Care Act 1980, for instance, has seven. Each part has its own descriptive title, in bold type, and may have a subtitle, in italics. These parts collect together Sections, which are numbered consecutively throughout the Act. There are ninety-one sections in the Child Care Act 1980. Again, each section has a short descriptive title. The Arrangement of Sections is followed by the *Preamble* which defines the general scope of the Act. The Child Care Act 1980 is 'An Act to consolidate certain enactments relating to the care of children by local authorities or voluntary organisations and certain other enactments relating to care of children'. At the end of the preamble, in square brackets, is the date on which the Act received the Royal Assent and became law, in this case 31 January 1980.

The date of Royal Assent is *not* necessarily the date when the Act comes into effect. This date, the Commencement, will always be found in one of the very last sections. In fact, it is quite common for this section simply to give a minister the power to make a statutory order as to when the Act will commence or indeed to bring different sections into use at different times. The Child Care Act 1980 was the subject of the Child Care Act 1980 (Commencement) Order 1980, which set 1 April 1981 as the date when the whole Act would come into effect.

Following the preamble, the various sections are printed. They may be further divided into subsections by the use of letters or numerals. A reference to s. 3(1)(b)(i) of the Child Care Act 1980 takes the reader to a specific phrase in subsection 1b of section 3, for instance. The last few sections of Acts are relatively standard. We have already referred to the commencement provision, but there are generally also sections dealing with the interpretation of specific terms, with the extent to which the Act applies throughout the United Kingdom, with transitional arrangements and repeals, and with a recognized short title. These final sections are followed by Schedules which elaborate upon specific sections in the Act. The Child Care Act has six schedules. Two of these deal with the membership of Children's Regional Planning Committees, which coordinate residential care provision, and Appeal Tribunals, dealing with refusals to register voluntary homes. Others spell out the transitional provisions as the Act comes into effect, arrangements for cases which involve people resident in Scotland or Northern Ireland, and the amendments and repeals of previous legislation.

If it is necessary to look up original legislation, it is often, in fact, more sensible not to go to the Act itself but to one of the commercial publications which reprint current legislation with accompanying explanatory notes. The standard source in this area is a volume called *Clarke Hall and Morrison on Children* which was last revised to March 1981. More recent measures can be found in *Current Law Statutes* (London: Sweet and Maxwell/Stevens) which reprints and comments on Acts within a short period of the Royal Assent being given.

Child Care Act 1980

The Child Care Act 1980 consolidates a number of earlier statutes as part of a continuing programme of legal rationalization intended to reduce the number of separate pieces of legislation that need to be referred to on any given topic. For our present purposes, its most important sections are those which relate to the voluntary reception of children into care, their detention against parental requests for return, and their treatment once in care. In general, these sections derive from the Children Act 1948 and its reformulation of a body of poor law provisions which themselves build on the historic obligations of local parishes going back at least to Tudor times. These developments rest on a view of the state as a guardian of last resort for those children whose parents are unwilling or unable to care for them adequately. Over the years, the scope of this intervention has enlarged and its spirit become somewhat more positive, but the underlying principles are of considerable antiquity. Today this Act provides the most commonly used legal basis for children coming into care, about seventy per cent of all admissions in recent years.

Paradoxically, perhaps, the Act begins by enjoining local authorities to avoid bringing children into care. Section 1(1) states:

> It shall be the duty of every local authority to make available such advice, guidance and assistance as may promote the welfare of children by diminishing the need to receive children into or keep them in care under this Act or to bring children before a juvenile court; and any provisions made by a local authority under this. subsection may, if the local authority think fit, include provision for giving assistance in kind or, in exceptional circumstances, in cash.

It is statements like this that justify our reference to the local authority as a 'guardian of last resort'. Wherever possible, children are to be kept out of care, and wide powers are made available to this end. Over the years, this provision has been used to fund a remarkable variety of programmes intended to help children at risk, whether of abuse, delinquency, truancy or any other hazard. Nowadays, unfortunately, the financial constraints on local authorities make it much less effective. In some areas any significant item of expenditure requires the personal approval of the Director of Social Services, and almost everywhere such discretion as local staff ever enjoyed has been eroded by inflation and accounting restrictions.

Nevertheless, it is not always possible to keep children out of care and section 2 of the Act spells out a 'duty . . . to provide for orphans, deserted children, etc.':

> Where it appears to a local authority with respect to a child in their area appearing to them to be under the age of seventeen –
>
> (a) that he has neither parent nor guardian or has been and remains abandoned by his parents or guardian or is lost; or
> (b) that his parents or guardian are, for the time being or permanently, prevented by reason of mental or bodily disease or infirmity or other incapacity or any other circumstances from providing for his proper accommodation, maintenance and upbringing; and
> (c) in either case, that the intervention of the local authority is necessary in the interests of the welfare of the child, it shall be the duty of the local authority to receive the child into their care under this section. (s. 2(1))

The section goes on to place the authority under a duty to keep the child in care until the age of eighteen as long as his or her welfare seems to require this (s. 2(2)). On the other hand, the authority may not detain the child if his or her parent or guardian wants to take over the responsibility for care and must, where consistent with the child's welfare, attempt to secure that care is taken over by a parent, guardian, relative or friend (s. 2(3)).

Where there is no alternative caretaker, then, the local authority must assume this duty. However, if the child's parents or guardian wish to resume a caretaking role, the local authority must, in principle, permit them to do so. It is in this sense that we can talk of the Act as allowing voluntary reception into care. The reception is not voluntary in the sense that parents must request it or, indeed, that the authority must obtain the sort of informed consent which precedes medical treatment. Although parents are commonly asked to sign various agreements to reception, and this would seem to be good practice, these have no legal force. Again, there are various loopholes which the authority may use to restrict its interpretation of its duty under the Act when resources are tight. The criteria for the child's welfare, in determining whether he or she should be received under section 2(1)(c), kept under section 2(2) or discharged under section 2(3), are flexible. Even so the authority must stand ready to defend its decision in terms of these statutory obligations.

Section 3 Resolutions

It should be apparent that a conflict can arise between the duty, in section 2(2), to keep a child in care as long as his or her welfare requires and the obligation to return the child if requested. This is the situation which section 3 of the Act deals with, specifying certain circumstances in which the local authority may detain the child in care. The procedure is for the authority, or more usually its social services committee acting under delegated powers, to pass a resolution that parental rights be assumed in respect of a named child. The committee must be given sufficient information, usually in a short written report prepared by the social services department, to be satisfied that the child's circumstances fall within criteria defined in subsection 3(1) which we discuss below. For this reason, the report will often be seen in advance by the authority's solicitors department, to check its legal validity. A resolution is then formally moved and minuted. Each parent must be the subject of a separate resolution.

Once a resolution has been passed, notice must be served on the parent named in it, who then has twenty-eight days in which to object, in writing, to the authority. Within fourteen days of receiving the objection, the authority must file an application to uphold the resolution with the juvenile court or it will automatically lapse. The application will lead to a court hearing where the local authority has to satisfy the magistrates that grounds exist for taking over parental rights and that it is in the child's interest to do so.

The grounds on which resolutions may be passed, and which the court will look to in any hearing, are specified in subsection 3(1). We can consider each of these in turn and note the sort of evidence which would be needed for the court to uphold a Section 3 resolution. By implication, it is obviously good practice to ensure that this evidence is available before attempting to pass the original resolution.

Grounds for passing resolutions are as follows:

(a) that his parents are dead and he has no guardian or custodian;

In the nature of things, this is unlikely to come before the courts. Nevertheless, proof of the parents' deaths should be available to the social services committee so that they may be properly satisfied that the ground is established before passing their resolution.

(b) that a parent of his –
 (i) has abandoned him.

'Abandonment' has two senses here. There is the general meaning of leaving a child to his or her fate and a special meaning, under subsection 3(8), of the parent's whereabouts being unknown to the authority for a period of twelve months. (Section 9 of the Act requires parents to keep the authority notified of their address while their child is in care.)

(ii) suffers from some permanent disability rendering him incapable of caring for the child, or
(iii) while not falling within sub-paragraph (ii) of this paragraph, suffers from a mental disorder (within the meaning of the Mental Health Act 1959), which renders him unfit to have the care of the child.

Both of these grounds will obviously require appropriate medical evidence to be available. It should be noted that a mental disorder does not have to be permanent in nature for the ground to be met. This relaxation recognizes the difficulty of prediction in the field of psychiatric illness and should allow for a concentration on the present hazards to the child. In both of these clauses, and those that follow, the 'care of the child' takes in emotional and mental, as well as physical, wellbeing. There is, however, a contrast with the comparable provisions in the Children and Young Persons Act 1969, in that it is not necessary to establish that harm has actually occurred to the child. Preventive action is, therefore, permissible.

> (iv) is of such habits or mode of life as to be unfit to have the care of the child.

Here we come onto a more contentious area. The standard law texts have an almost Victorian ring, with phrases like 'vagrancy, habitual inebriety, immoral, vicious or criminal conduct'. As such, there is obviously room for debate on the degree to which, for instance, being an itinerant worker, a registered drug addict or a prostitute actually impairs the capacity for child care, in the broad sense already outlined. If the Section 3 procedure is to be any more than a judgement about morals here, the most appropriate line to take would probably be to start from the child's condition at the point of reception into care, in the context of the family history, and then consider whether there had been any significant subsequent change in the parent's conduct. The courts have ruled that resolutions on this ground cannot rely on a single act but require evidence of repeated behaviour. On the other hand, evidence as to a parent's past history and any criminal record is admissible in proving the case, unlike the traditional practice in criminal proceedings.

> (v) has so consistently failed without reasonable cause to discharge the obligations of a parent as to be unfit to have the care of the child;

As we have noted, parents of children in care have a statutory obligation to keep the authority notified of their whereabouts and they must also pay maintenance contributions (ss. 45–55). There is too, an implied obligation to maintain contact with the

child by means of visits, letters, cards, telephone calls or whatever. If the parent's circumstances improve, but he or she does
not indicate a willingness to have the child back, this may also
be relevant. Any legal move is, again, likely to rest both on the
history of parental acts and on attitudes over the period the child
has been in care. As with 'habits', the idea of actions through
time is important. The courts have tended to interpret this
ground very restrictively. It may be necessary to establish that
not only have the parents not shown willingness to discharge
their obligations but that they have, in the words of one judge,
shown a 'callous disregard' for their children. This ground is a
deceptively difficult one to establish.

> (c) that a resolution under paragraph (b) of this subsection is in
> force in relation to one parent of the child who is, or is likely to
> become, a member of the household comprising the child and
> his other parent;

Subsection (c) is an equivalent of the 'same household' ground
in care proceedings where there is evidence of one parent consti-
tuting some hazard to a child, but no evidence against the other.
Since rights must be assumed for each parent separately, the
absence of evidence against the other parent could otherwise
pose legal problems. It would, for instance, be possible for that
parent to request the child's discharge back to a setting from
which the authority was anxious to protect him or her.

> (d) that throughout the three years preceding the passing of the
> resolution, the child has been in the care of a local authority
> under Section 2 of this Act, or partly in the care of a local
> authority and partly in the care of a voluntary organisation.

This final ground is designed to allow local authorities to act
more positively in the case of children who have drifted into
long-term care, where parents may have little real prospect of
resuming care of their children but are obstructing more satisfactory placements such as fostering rather than institutional
care. It should ensure that the social, emotional and psychological relationships formed by a child in substitute care are not

precipitately disrupted by a request for his or her discharge. Its proof is a simple matter of fact, although of course the social services committee, and the court, must be satisfied that the child's interests are served by assuming parental rights.

When should this procedure be used? The Child Care Act 1980 restates the powers of the Secretary of State to make regulations for the conduct of reviews of children in care. At present, the Boarding-Out of Children Regulations 1955 remain in force. Among other provisions, these place a duty on local authorities to review the cases of all children in their care at least once every six months. Although there is great variation in the diligence of authorities' attention to this duty, in the absence of any effective enforcement, it would seem to be good practice to consider the assumption of rights on all children on each occasion. In our view, once a child has been in care for three years, there should be a clear presumption that parental rights will be assumed unless there are compelling reasons to the contrary. This need not preclude an eventual return of the child, although Tizard's research in *Adoption: A Second Chance* (London: Open Books, 1977), would seem to suggest that this is rarely in the child's interest after such a lapse of time. Given the findings by Rowe and Lambert in *Children Who Wait* (London: Association of British Adoption Agencies, 1973), which indicated that, once a child had been in care for more than six months, he or she had only a one in four likelihood of returning to his or her own family, it seems arguable that, if evidence exists, the assumption of parental rights should be seriously considered well before three years have elapsed.

Section 3 is not well suited to use as an emergency procedure. Since the Act refers specifically to a resolution being passed, this is not a power which can be delegated to the Director of Social Services. Its operation will require some involvement by social services committee members with properly delegated authority to act. Once the parent has requested the child's return, the propriety of a Section 3 resolution becomes suspect, although the local authority's position has been strengthened by a recent (1980) case in the House of Lords, *Lewisham London Borough* v. *Lewisham Juvenile Court*. This held that authorities retained the power to pass Section 3 resolutions after a parental request for the return of a child, provided that they did so before the child was actually transferred to the parent's care. If that gap between request and return is to be long enough for the procedure to operate, staff may find themselves engaged in delaying tactics which can only sour relations with parents and invite censure. In some rural areas, for instance, social workers can take advantage of the fact that the authority is only obliged to allow the parents to collect their child, and rely on transport difficulties obstructing their attempts to do so. As soon as the child is actually transferred to his or her parents, the authority's power ceases and any action must now take place under a different statute.

It seems better, then to anticipate such situations by considering the possibility of a Section 3 resolution whenever a child in voluntary care is the subject of a formal case review. Some people may prefer to avoid this, for fear of stirring up quiescent parents. On the other hand, if a resolution allows the child's future to be secured as a result of an unhurried consideration of his or her circumstances, rather than as a panic response to parental pressure, it does seem desirable to take the opportunity if it is presented. Section 3 resolutions do seem appropriate, though, as the routine response to certain types of emergency, like the abandonment of a child in a public place. Where a baby has been left, for instance, it must be received into care under section 2 and assumption of parental rights should follow swiftly as an effective means of securing the child. If a person claiming to be a parent subsequently comes forward, the authority can investigate the claim and exercise its own discretion over whether the child's interests will be best served by being returned.

This procedure also has advantages for parents. In contrast to their limited legal standing in care proceedings, which we shall describe later, they are full parties to any subsequent legal action. Specifically, this means that they are able to obtain legal aid for representation of their interests before the magistrates, to call evidence on their own behalf and to examine the local authority's case. Parents also have a more clearly recognized right of appeal to the Family Division of the High Court, with its specialized expertise in child care issues. Local authorities enjoy the same right under this section.

Once a child has been in care for more than six months, his or her parents must give the local authority twenty-eight days' notice of their desire to resume care of the child. During this period, the local authority may still assume parental rights. If this notice is not given, or if the child is induced or assisted to run away, taken without lawful authority, or harboured, the adults involved are guilty of a criminal offence and may be fined up to four hundred pounds or imprisoned for up to three months or both (s. 13). If a person is known to be harbouring the child, a magistrate may be asked to issue a summons requiring the child to be produced in court within a specified period, upon a penalty of one hundred pounds' fine or two months' imprisonment or both. Alternatively, the magistrate can issue a warrant to an officer of the local authority authorizing him to search named premises and remove the child (s. 15). The same provisions apply to children on care orders, but with the important difference that they operate throughout the United Kingdom and the Channel Islands. Children in voluntary care may only be recovered within England and Wales.

We should not, however, overstress the compulsory elements of this Act, despite their great importance in providing a secure and stable basis for the protection of children in need of care. If we look at England and Wales, in the year ending 31 March 1978, for instance, fifty-three per cent of children in voluntary care left within eight weeks and nearly seventy per cent in less than six months. Although sixty-nine per cent of admissions were under this statute, this only represented forty-six per cent of all children in care at any one time. Of these, only thirty-eight per cent had had parental rights assumed (17.7 thousand children). The commonest cause of admission is the short-term illness of a parent or guardian. About 0.25 per cent of children under eighteen were admitted and just over 0.35 per cent were actually in care at a given date.

Family Proceedings

This section groups together a miscellany of proceedings under several different Acts which may result in a child coming into care. Technically, these admissions result from orders committing a child to care which are different from care orders, in that the child remains the ultimate responsibility of the court rather than the local authority. There are five main provisions: where an adoption order is refused (Children Act 1975, s. 17(1)(b)); where custody is contested in divorce proceedings (Matrimonial Causes Act 1973, s. 43); as a result of guardianship applications (Guardianship Act 1973, s. 2(2)(b)); through matrimonial proceedings in magistrates' courts, dealing with separation, maintenance and custody (Domestic Proceedings and Magistrates' Courts Act 1978, s. 10); and in wardship proceedings (Family Law Reform Act 1969, s. 7(4)). If the custodianship provisions of the Children Act 1975, allowing caretakers other than parents or local authorities to apply for legal custody of a child, ever come into effect, a sixth provision will become available under section 36.

Altogether, these various orders brought fewer than a thousand children into care in the year ending 31 March 1978. For most of them, the main usefulness is on occasions when concern is aroused for a child's welfare and the proceedings are already in train or actively contemplated. The courts have ruled in matrimonial matters that the local authority can have an interest and, therefore, apply to become a party to the action, and it seems reasonable to suppose that the same principle would be followed in other proceedings. By comparison with care proceedings, they are procedurally cumbersome and expensive, although the parents' status is somewhat stronger. Legal aid is more readily available and it is easier to get a subsequent review of the local authority's handling of a particular child in care. Technically, the local authority is only acting as the court's agent in caring for a child, so that the court can be asked to rule on the appropriateness of any of the authority's decisions. Given the legal complexities, family proceedings are only likely to be relevant where other parties have already initiated them, as parents filing a petition for divorce, or where issues are very finely balanced and do not fall easily into the criteria set out in either the Child Care Act 1980 or the Children and Young Persons Act 1969. There is a large area of judicial discretion, since the 'first and paramount consideration' (Guardianship of Minors Act 1971, s. 1) is the welfare of the child rather than the application of specific tests.

This flexibility becomes of great significance in the one exception to these rather dismissive-sounding remarks – wardship proceedings. Some people have been very excited by their possible relevance in care matters and have received a certain amount of encouragement from the judges of the Family Division. The proceedings are seen as a way of getting a fuller hearing of cases than is possible in the juvenile court, with less attention to statutory limitations and more to the child's welfare. On the other hand, wardship proceedings raise a good many issues of a technical legal nature and should only be contemplated after close consideration by the social services' legal advisers. In many, if not most, cases, simpler and cheaper procedures will achieve effectively the same result.

The essence of wardship is that, once a child becomes a ward of court, all important issues respecting that child become subject to the direction of the High Court. Furthermore, a child can be made a ward of court rapidly and easily. The moment the summons is issued by the court, the child becomes a ward and subject to its jurisdiction. This can be done in a matter of hours if the lawyers are familiar with the procedure. However, efforts must be made to bring up the case before a judge as soon as possible. An appointment with a registrar of the High Court must be made within twenty-one days of the issue of the summons, and if this is not done the child will cease to be a ward at the end of that period. The registrar, though, may find it difficult to fix an early date for a hearing of the issues. Much depends on where the case arises. The judge should be a member of the Family Division of the High Court (although Deputy Judges may hear these cases), and in some parts of the country it can be a considerable time before an appropriate judge is available. Elsewhere, especially in London, a date for a hearing can be arranged very rapidly.

Wardship is an ancient common law jurisdiction. There are few statutes which affect its operation and judges enjoy a wide discretion in the conduct of hearings, the recognition of interested parties and the orders which they can make. The basic test is: what is in the best interests of the child? This contrasts sharply with the close definitions in section 3 of the Child Care Act 1980, already discussed, and section 1 of the Children and Young Persons Act 1969, which we shall examine in the next chapter. A judge can, for example, make an order under the wardship jurisdiction that a child be removed from its parents before any harm should come to it simply because the judge considers that this would be in the child's best interests. While this power may be useful in protecting children, it can readily be seen what great scope it confers on judges to intervene in family life for no more precise reason than that they feel that the child's interests are best served that way. Further, in the absence of any clearly defined limit to the range of orders which judges can make, they could, for example, require certain people to refrain from visiting the child. In this way a child could be kept at home but a person who was considered a potential threat to the child ordered to stay away from there. This result can be achieved indirectly under a care order, but could not be specified by a magistrates' court in making such an order.

In wardship cases a judge can also order that a child should not be moved from its present environment without the consent of the court, and orders could even be made specifying what is to be done concerning the child's education or health. Contravention of such orders can be punished by immediate, and indefinite, imprisonment for contempt of court. Wardship can also be used as a response to parental harassment of a local authority. One example has involved the small stepson of a man who had a substantial criminal record for indecency with children. This child was the subject of care proceedings under the 1969 Act and a care order was made. His stepfather applied for its revocation every six months, as was his legal right. The effect, however, was to involve the authority in almost continuous litigation and destabilize their planning for the child. After six applications had been defeated, the local authority filed a successful application for wardship, so that no further attempt at revocation could begin without the High Court's consent.

These may all seem substantial advantages to a local authority, and may appear to suggest that wardship proceedings might frequently be more useful to them than care proceedings. However, a number of points must be borne in mind when thinking of wardship as an alternative. Perhaps most importantly, a child can be committed into the care of a local authority in wardship proceedings only if there are exceptional circumstances making it impracticable or undesirable for it to continue to be under the care of his parents or of any other individual (Family Law Reform Act 1969, s. 7(2)). This may not, in fact, be a very great restriction on the judge's power to commit a child into care, because judges are likely to find that exceptional circumstances exist if that is what they want to do. More importantly, if a child is committed into care in this way, the High Court retains a continuing jurisdiction over the child, so that if the authority and the parents disagree about anything, it is always open to the parents to go back to the High Court for directions. Similarly, the authority should not take any important decision about the child (for example, whether to move him from short to long-stay foster parents, or to go home on trial) without the permission of the court. These are all substantial limitations in the power of the authority compared to their position under a care order. Finally, instead of committing the child into care, the judge may simply grant its *care and control* to the local authority. This is a somewhat technical distinction, but its effect is that the authority has even less control over the child than if he or she is committed into care under these proceedings, for the child is not technically in its care at all, and doubts may arise about the legality of contributing to his or her maintenance.

Wardship proceedings have a number of characteristics which are very different from those in juvenile court. The latter proceedings, as we shall see, are entirely oral: that is, the evidence must (with very limited exceptions) be given verbally by witnesses in open court. The home surroundings report is usually the only written document which is presented to the court (unless an independent person has been appointed as a *guardian ad litem* for the child's interests – see chapter 7). But in wardship proceedings the case will often be substantially presented to the judge in the form of affidavits, sworn statements by relevant persons. In general, these will be available to all parties to the case, although the judge does have a discretion to receive and consider them in confidence. An affidavit, if taken from a social worker, may contain very much the same kinds of contents as a home surroundings report. This means that a judge can have before him written documents which may be based on hearsay evidence and which may contain many statements of opinion. He may even order the production of other documents, a power not possessed by magistrates. It seems to be accepted that the strict rules of evidence do not apply in wardship proceedings, and some local authority lawyers see this as an advantage because in this way they can present as evidence material which could not so easily be placed before a juvenile court. On the other hand, as we shall see, many juvenile courts take a fairly relaxed view of the rules of evidence, and the practical difference may not be very great, except where the local magistrates are particularly strict. Nevertheless, fieldworkers should not suppose that the admitted flexibility of wardship means that they can get away with a flimsy case. Witnesses can be cross-examined on their affidavits and the judge himself is likely to play a much more dominating role and to be prepared to follow up matters on which he does not feel happy. As we shall stress, in considering evidence in care proceedings, carefully recorded observations and opinions (where necessary) based on facts will always carry more weight than vague and unchecked statements.

Being in the High Court, representation in wardship proceedings must be by a barrister. This of course adds to the costs, which local authorities are unlikely to be keen to incur unless absolutely essential. A further complicating factor is that in some cases the court may call for reports by the Official Solicitor. The Official Solicitor's office is a small department situated in

London with special responsibilities to certain classes of litigants, especially people under disadvantage in litigation. This of course includes children. But his appointment will depend on a request by the court, which is probably made in about half of all wardship hearings. It should be remembered that the Official Solicitor is what his name says: a solicitor, and not a social worker. His staff are legally trained, although they are often thought to have developed a certain expertise in children's cases over the years. The length and thoroughness of their investigations will vary from case to case, but can add considerably to the time it takes for the matter to come before a judge. When it does so, the report of the Official Solicitor is made to the court, but will normally also be available to other parties, although the judge does have the power to withhold it from them if he thinks this is in the child's interests. The Official Solicitor will usually be represented in court by a barrister. The parents, and indeed any person with an interest in the proceedings, can be made a party to them (and receive legal aid for this), so that there could be quite an elaborate array of legal representatives in court.

Whatever the view of the local authority about the desirability of initiating wardship proceedings itself, it is always possible that such proceedings may be brought by parents (or others) with respect to a child who is in care or whom the authority is considering taking into care. Of course this will depend on the quality of legal advice given to the parents, and perhaps on their means, because it may not be as easy to obtain legal aid to institute wardship proceedings as it is to participate in them once they have been started by someone else. Nevertheless, if the child is already fully in the local authority's care, either because he or she has been committed into its care after care proceedings or because a resolution has been passed under section 3 of the Child Care Act 1980, the High Court will be most reluctant to use the wardship jurisdiction in such a way as to interfere with the authority's discretion in dealing with the child. So, for practical purposes, once those procedures have been invoked, there is little threat (to the authority) of the matter being taken outside the statutory provisions described earlier which relate to such procedures. But if the authority has not yet obtained parental rights over the child, as, for example, if the child is only *voluntarily* in care under section 2 of the Child Care Act 1980, then, if the child is made a ward of court, the matter will have to be dealt with fully under that jurisdiction.

Although there has been some increase in the popularity of wardship proceedings in recent years, then, they do remain relatively uncommon. On 31 March 1978 there were only about three hundred children in local authority care on this provision, with somewhere around one hundred orders having been made in the preceding twelve months. Many of their virtues do seem to depend upon their exceptional nature, and it may be as well to retain them for those rare circumstances in which a child's needs fall outside the scope of the provision of the 1980 and 1969 Acts. Certainly, wardship is not a provision which lends itself to routine usage.

This chapter, then, has explained the provisions of the Child Care Act 1980 on the circumstances in which local authorities must receive children into care, if it seems necessary for the child's welfare, and in which they may subsequently assume parental rights and detain children against their parents' will. It was stressed, however, that the first duty of local authorities was to prevent such receptions. We concluded by examining the varied provisions which could collectively be described as family proceedings, with particular reference to wardship. These were seen to have little to offer in most cases but to constitute a reservoir of powers which could sometimes be helpful. None of them should, however, be contemplated without further legal advice.

Chapter 4

The Grounds for Care Proceedings

A social worker who considers that care proceedings ought to be initiated must first satisfy herself that a court is likely to make the order which she seeks . . . She must therefore know precisely what the court will be looking for when deciding whether or not to make an order . . .

John George Auckland Inquiry   1975

The preceding chapter discussed two of the routes by which children might come into the care of local authorities. This was intended to furnish a context for any decision to embark on care proceedings. These are less common than voluntary receptions but substantially more contentious. They are also of considerable practical significance. Although care orders, whether in civil care or criminal proceedings, represent less than a third of all admissions to care, they contribute almost fifty per cent of children actually in care. In this chapter, we shall discuss the criteria set out by the Children and Young Persons Act 1969 and the circumstances in which they may be relevant. Once again, these should be seen as applying to all child protection agencies: local authorities have a duty, under section 2(1), to investigate any information suggesting that a *prima facie* case exists. Implicitly, one might argue for at least a moral obligation on other agencies to place information before the social services department if they have reason to suppose that a child's circumstances fall under one of the grounds specified in the act.

The Children and Young Persons Act 1969

In contrast to the line of legislative descent represented by the Child Care Act 1980, the antecedents of the Children and Young Persons Act 1969 go back only as far as the nineteenth century. This series of enactments, rather than reflecting the residual role of the state as a guardian of last resort, define a set of occasions in which it might be appropriate for the state actively to intervene and displace parents from their status as children's caretakers. Those occasions are laid down in section 1(2) of the 1969 Act, which unites five separate legislative strands: the proper development and same household grounds (a, b and bb); the moral danger ground (c); the beyond control ground (d); the truancy ground (e); and the offence ground (f). In all cases, a second test has to be met, namely that without a court order the child will not receive the care or control thought to be necessary.

Most of these conditions relate to things which the child has done or might do. In this sense, the 1969 Act is partly concerned with the social *control* of children. Some conditions relate to things which others have done or might do to the child. Here, the statute provides means to the social *care* of children. Alternatively, we can invert the approach, by relying more heavily on the second test, to see the primary conditions as a set of entitlements or rights which all children should expect to enjoy – adequate conditions for growth and development, protection from ill-treatment or moral danger, regular schooling and sufficient supervision to prevent the child from committing deviant acts until he or she is of an age to make responsible choices and accept the consequences. In this version, care proceedings would be a documentation of *parental* failure.

Historically, these different emphases relate to attempts to realize distinct policy objectives: the protection of persons or property from actual or potential delinquency (child control); the prevention of inhumane acts against children (child care); and the promotion of children's welfare as a national investment (parental monitoring). Many otherwise puzzling features of the 1969 Act result from its ill-considered attempt to reconcile all three goals within a single framework of social and legal institutions.

Care proceedings are subject to the overriding principle of section 1 of the 1980 Act, already discussed, that taking children into care should be avoided so far as possible, consistent with the child's welfare. At the same time, if inquiries have established the existence of a *prima facie* case, the authority has a duty to bring it before the court, unless they are satisfied this is not in the child's or the public interest or that some other person is about to do so (s. 2(2)). If it is considered necessary to institute proceedings, a juvenile court will ultimately have to be satisfied both that one or more of the specified conditions applies and that a court order is necessary to meet a need for care or control. By implication, the specified conditions guide all agencies in what constitutes a legitimate cause for concern about a child's welfare and indicate the sort of considerations which should operate in assessing a case and the relevance of legal intervention. We shall, therefore, consider each of the seven conditions in some detail.

Local authorities and, in some cases, the police or the NSPCC may intervene to take a child into care on the grounds that:

(a) his proper development is being avoidably prevented or neglected or his health is being avoidably impaired or neglected or he is being ill-treated;

This is the ground on which most proceedings relating to child abuse or neglect are brought. It is convenient, then, to separate it into two parts for the purposes of exposition, although in any particular case both may well apply. In practice, it is very difficult to draw a line between abused and neglected children.

The first two phrases relate primarily to neglect, but in slightly different ways. The distinction between 'proper development' and 'health' seems to imply that the former covers more than the simple physical wellbeing of the child. Proper development can reasonably be considered to include psychological, emotional or mental elements as much as those relating to height, weight, motor skills or whatever. Most courts will accept this, provided that adequate evidence is produced, a point to which we shall return. Often, of course, physical signs will accompany impairments to psychological aspects of development. On the other hand, there have been occasional cases of parents who subscribe to theories of 'natural development' who have brought their children up in an otherwise affectionate environment, caring adequately for their physical needs, but refraining from any attempt to give positive stimulation or structure to their behaviour. A somewhat similar case might be of parents with particular moral beliefs who may be caring, loving and stimulating towards their children but who also insist on their isolation from a society which they, the parents, consider to be essentially corrupt. It must be stressed, however, that these situations are rare. Most commonly, a child's proper development is being adversely affected by a low level of parental competence, for whatever reason, rather than an articulated set of alternative principles for living.

Some people might interpret health in a similarly broad fashion, especially if one follows the World Health Organization's definition of the term as 'a complete state of physical, mental and social wellbeing'. However, it seems more conventionally to be applied in circumstances where parents or caretakers are acting contrary to medical advice with demonstrably harmful effects on their child. This situation might arise where, as in cases of epilepsy or severe asthma, a child's health is dependent upon regular medication which the parent is failing to administer. Similarly, aspects of caretaking may pose health hazards, as when irregular changing of nappies causes severe rashes and skin infections which may lead to permanent scarring. Another example might be where poor hygiene with feeding gives rise to frequent gastro-intestinal infections, some of which can be life-threatening. The commonest causes, again, are low levels of parental competence, although there are occasional cases of principled unorthodox child-rearing. A number of children whose parents have followed macrobiotic diets, for instance, have developed dietary deficiency conditions, and proceedings have occasionally been thought necessary. This procedure, however, is not recommended where consent to life-saving surgery or blood transfusion is withheld on religious grounds, most commonly by Jehovah's Witnesses. Central government guidance, in Ministry of Health Circular F/P9/1B and Home Office Circular 63/1968, is that this is an inappropriate use of the legislation, although the circulars do predate the present Act. In this situation, doctors are advised to obtain a second medical opinion confirming the necessity of the intervention and then to proceed on the basis of their own professional conscience.

Although we should not be misled by the rare case of principled dissent into ignoring the common incapacity, neither should we shirk the difficult moral issue of the right of public agencies to impose particular standards of family life. For better or worse, we as a society have determined that children, whether in our interests or theirs, should be protected from certain sorts of conduct which we consider potentially harmful. In order to achieve this objective we have created a number of agencies in health, education, social work and law who are funded to seek out and prevent such harms. We have, in effect, set limits to our tolerance of dissent, whether active or passive. These are broad limits: neither proper development nor health is a discrete state of being, so much as a range of normal variation. What agency personnel are directed to consider, however, is the state of the child rather than the beliefs of the parents. If those beliefs, implemented in child-rearing practices, are having an identifiable adverse affect on the child, then intervention is potentially justifiable. Once the child is of an age to decide for himself or herself, then the justification for intervention is much weakened. The responsibility of the public agencies is to ensure that the child's wellbeing does not suffer any lasting impairment before the child is capable of making informed choices, and accepting consequential hazards.

We must also recognize that proper development and health are relative notions. They are tied to the condition of the particular child in question. What this implies is a duty to look at the child's individual potential and how far it is being achieved. This can be particularly important with subnormal or sickly children where there is a risk of deciding that, if the child's potential is inevitably limited, deficit is not a matter to worry about unduly. It could also be relevant, however, for a child of average potential born to mentally or sensorily handicapped parents. In part, this is covered by the use of the word 'avoidably'. The harm caused to the child does not have to result from intentional acts. Parents can be making the best of limited capacities but, set against some notion of what the child might expect from averagely competent parents, still be failing to a degree that is having serious and lasting adverse effects on the child.

The ill-treatment element is rather more straightforward. This relates to the classic instances of child abuse where children have been subject to acts of cruelty by parents or caretakers. One problem which often arises, though, is over the boundary between reasonable, if zealous, chastisement and ill-treatment. Parents are regularly surprised to find that what they consider to be necessary and appropriate correction is adjudged ill-treatment. It is unlikely that any court would accept an application based solely on the fact that a parent used physical means of punishment. Hitting children is not, in itself, an illegal act in this country. On the other hand, it does seem that any blow which causes more than temporary discomfort could potentially constitute ill-treatment, especially if bruising results or the skin is broken. Similarly, if otherwise unobjectionable punishments are accompanied by an element of ritual sadism, this could raise questions about the effects on the child's psychological development which would justify proceedings.

Two points need to be made in relation to the whole of this ground. The first is that it is phrased entirely in the present tense. There are two implications. On the one hand, there could be difficulties if the proceedings are in relation to a child who has been ill-treated, etc., but who is now in a safe place, e.g. a hospital or with foster-parents. This may sound a somewhat specious argument, but lawyers sometimes advance it, although, in general, courts take a commonsense attitude and it is unlikely that an application would be dismissed on that basis. The other implication is that this ground does not cover feared future harms. This is unlike the situation in Scotland, for instance, where section 32(2) of the Social Work (Scotland) Act 1968 permits proceedings where 'lack of parental care . . . *is likely to* cause [the child] unnecessary suffering or seriously to impair his health or development' (our emphasis). Some courts will, nonetheless, accept cases where harm is anticipated, such as those of children removed at birth from women with certain serious mental disorders. It might just be possible to stretch the notion of proper development to cover this by claiming that 'development' is a continuing process and that the very subjection of a child to an environment where it is at risk of injury is in itself an impairment of its proper development. But there is inevitably likely to be an undue element of speculation in any such argument and, in our view, any attempt to use this ground preventively is of doubtful legality, unless the case comes within the provisions (b) or (bb) discussed below. If it does not, it seems that wardship is probably a more satisfactory way of proceeding in such circumstances, and many local authority lawyers are likely to take this view.

The second general point is that substantiating any of these conditions is likely to involve health service personnel, wherever the concern originates. It must be recognized that they are more likely to identify children as candidates for intervention on this ground because much of their work consists of the detailed scrutiny of individuals' growth and development. This is particularly true in community health services but is also an increasingly important element of both paediatrics and general practice. Such a purely technical foundation is lacking in social work, teaching or police work. If a case is to be made out at all, though, it will be necessary to include evidence of the child's physical condition which can only be furnished by someone with an appropriate background. Given the references to 'avoidable' impairment, it will, of course, also be essential to rule out any possible organic cause. In court, generally speaking, such evidence will have to come from a doctor, although in some cases a suitably experienced health visitor might, if thought appropriate, be able to provide it.

We have analysed this section in a way which has tended to

separate abuse and neglect and, to some degree, emphasized the more principled types of parental failure. Before moving on, however, we should stress that the most common types of case do not involve explicit assertions of principle nor do they distinguish sharply elements of abuse or neglect. The largest areas of concern are for children who are undersized, poorly stimulated, given to frequent minor illnesses and prone to collecting trivial cuts and bruises which do not seem to be accidental. For a variety of reasons proportionately few of these children ever come before a court, but they still outnumber the infinitesimal groups of children who suffer from calculated sadism or parental eccentricity. It is, of course, on this large grey margin of concern that the judgements on intervention are most finely balanced.

interesting

(b) It is probable that the condition set out in the preceding paragraph will be satisfied in his case, having regard to the fact that the court or another court has found that that condition is or was satisfied in the case of another child or young person who is or was a member of the household to which he belongs;

This ground has a preventive intent. What it does is to permit applications for an order on other children in a household where one child has been found to fall within the scope of the proper development ground. There is some danger of this being regarded as a rubber stamp by both courts and child protection agencies. Once one child has been abused or neglected, others may be removed more readily. Certainly this is an easier test than the one previously discussed, but it should be noted that the courts must still be satisfied of the probability of harm resulting to children who are the subject of applications under this subsection. The 'Cinderella syndrome', where one child is neglected or abused while others are well cared for, is not common but does occur. Good practice should require that the condition and circumstances of each child be considered separately, although of course the actual evidence may be substantially the same and be aggregated into a single set of proceedings.

There are some possible pitfalls in the wording of this ground. The phrase about the court or another court having found the proper development condition to be satisfied in the case of another child does not prevent simultaneous applications where one or more children in a household come under that condition and the remainder under the present condition. If the court accepts the former application, it may go on, within the same hearing, to consider the latter. Moreover, it is not essential for an application under the proper development condition to have been made. This circumstance may arise if a child has died from neglect or abuse, whether or not there has been a criminal conviction of his or her parents or caretakers. Evidence as to that child's treatment can be advanced and, if found to satisfy the proper development ground, an order under the present ground may be made in respect of the surviving children. There may, of course, be a gap in time between applications. Thus cases have arisen where, one child having been abused or neglected and been subject to an order on the proper development ground, children born subsequently to the same household have immediately become the subject of applications under this paragraph.

One rather grey area is the meaning of the word 'household'. This has never been legally defined in child welfare legislation and has a variety of senses in other areas. There could be difficulties in the case of children who were frequent visitors to a household where abuse had occurred. What we have in mind here is the possibility of a couple living together with children by their present relationship and other children from previous relationships regularly staying with them under divorce settlements. If any of the children were to be abused a problem could arise. Should the victim be a 'resident', then it might be possible to restrict the 'visitors' under matrimonial jurisdiction, which we mentioned in the previous chapter. If the victim is a 'visitor', it could be difficult to act in respect of 'resident' children under this condition. Much would depend on the attitude of the local court and its commonsense understanding of a household, but this might be an occasion to consider wardship. This issue could also affect the next ground.

(bb) it is probable that the conditions set out in paragraph (a) of this subsection will be satisfied in his case, having regard to the fact that a person who has been convicted of an offence mentioned in Schedule 1 to the Act of 1933 is, or may become, a member of the same household as the child;

This paragraph also has a preventive intent and was added by the Children Act 1975. The DHSS circular LASS 75/21 suggested that it would be appropriate to consider it where it could not be shown that a child had been persistently ill-treated but where there had been a number of instances of ill-treatment leading to the conviction of a caretaker and it was felt that the child was unlikely to be able to live satisfactorily with that adult. We think that this is unduly restrictive. The proper development ground makes no reference to *persistent* ill-treatment, unlike, say, section 3(1)(b)(v) of the 1980 Act, and is quite adequate to cover the situation envisaged by the circular.

What this ground is actually used for is to restrict the access of known offenders to children. Schedule 1 of the Children and Young Persons Act 1933 as amended by the Sexual Offences Act 1956 lists a number of criminal offences covered by special provisions, which need not concern us here. The list includes the murder or manslaughter of a child or young person, infanticide, abandonment, common or aggravated assault, abduction, procuring, unlawful sexual intercourse, incest, indecent assault and buggery, attempts to commit any of the foregoing or assisting others in committing those offences, or any other offence involving bodily injury to a child or young person. Thus if an adult has been convicted of one of these offences, and is thought to represent a hazard to children in the household, an application may be made for an order relating to the children. This would apply even if the victim child was not a member of the same household. This paragraph also opens up the possibility of applying for an order in anticipation of a known offender becoming a member of the household. This can be considered, for instance, where men with past convictions become engaged to single mothers with children from previous relationships. More often, of course, proceedings are used as a bargaining counter in such situations in attempts to persuade the parties voluntarily to reconsider the proposed cohabitation or marriage, but they are available as a last resort.

As in the previous ground, it is important to avoid regarding this as an occasion for rubber-stamping. The wording of the Act quite clearly directs the agencies to be suspicious of offenders, but it does require establishing a probability of harm under the proper development condition. This does not necessarily follow merely from the fact that an adult has a previous conviction. It may be that there is psychiatric evidence of a continuing incapacity to deal with children or of a low threshold of violence, particularly under the influence of drink or drugs. Another example is a case where a man convicted of a petty sexual offence against his cohabitee's daughter, and sentenced to a relatively short term of imprisonment, had written a number of erotic letters to the girl from prison. It was thought that these constituted evidence of possible harm in the future and that proceedings under this condition would be appropriate.

(c) he is exposed to moral danger;

This is also a preventive ground, but its sense has changed sharply in recent years. Its Victorian origins lay in attempts to prevent juveniles from acquiring delinquent values. A child who was regularly in the company of known criminals might be brought before the court for committal to an industrial school to learn the worth of thrift, honesty, diligence and similar virtues. Nowadays, however, it is almost exclusively concerned with attempts to prevent the sexual exploitation of girls. In 1978, 242 of the 280 successful applications on this condition were in respect of girls, 169 of whom were aged between fourteen and seventeen. This is a difficult area, and one in which many protection agencies feel increasingly uncertain. Although strictly illegal, there is widespread social tolerance of under-age sexual intercourse, at least for fourteen- and fifteen-year-olds, and it does seem that even the police are reluctant to intervene unless there are exploitative elements.

Where pregnancy results, however, this ground is worth

considering for preventive action in relation to the care of the baby. Proceedings against an under-age mother could offer a way of bringing both herself and the baby into an environment where her standards of child care could be supervised and developed.

In general, though, it is unlikely that precocious sexual activity is in itself sufficient to justify proceedings these days. One would probably need to establish that there was some element of coercion or deception or that the child was demonstrably incapable of understanding the implications of the acts in question and giving informed consent. There might also be circumstances where criminal prosecution of an adult would be inappropriate. It has, for instance, been argued that this is often the case with incest, and certain American states have experimented with partial decriminalization and a greater emphasis on family therapy. Where adults are prepared to cooperate in such a programme an application in care proceedings could offer a degree of security to a child victim while therapy proceeds. We must also recognize that there may be circumstances where no one is available for prosecution. Thus we have heard of occasions where children below the age of criminal responsibility have been procuring younger siblings. The procurer might be subject to proceedings on another condition, but this one could be available for the procured.

This section is also available for use where children are living with adults who have unorthodox sexual inclinations. As such, it has aroused a good deal of controversy, particularly when used to remove children from lesbian mothers. Here, again, we come to the difficult libertarian issues which are inherent in this whole area. The guiding principle should probably be the same: is there a demonstrable risk to the child? It would be an abuse of the legal process to turn care proceedings into a vehicle for persecuting homosexual parents for their homosexuality *per se*. On the other hand, intervention is clearly justifiable where a parent is seeking to impose his or her sexual preferences on a child, in circumstances where the child is clearly not free to make his or her own choice. This is an abuse of parental power and the law permits a check to be placed upon it.

Before leaving this condition, it is perhaps worth underlining that it need not be restricted to sexual matters. There are still occasions when children, especially those under the age of criminal responsibility, are enlisted by adults in the commission of offences. It may not always be either possible or appropriate to charge the child with a specific offence, and this condition still seems relevant. Another possibility is in relation to young children being sent out to beg in the streets. Parents or care-takers can be charged with a (Schedule 1) criminal offence in relation to this, under section 4 of the Children and Young Persons Act 1933, but this may not necessarily be desirable. Once again, care proceedings on the moral danger ground could be an option. The main point to bear in mind is that this ground does direct child protection agencies to examine the whole of a child's moral environment and not just its sexual aspects.

(d) he is beyond the control of his parent or guardian;

This condition is another Victorian legacy, but is now compara-tively uncommon. Under the age of fourteen it is most commonly encountered for boys (154 successful applications, to eighty-one for girls), while over fourteen the proportions are almost exactly reversed (104 for boys to 198 for girls). Implicit in this ground is the right of parents to command a degree of obedience from their children and the availability of support from public agencies in this task. Plainly, however, the breakdown in authority would have to be of a rather serious nature, such as to rule out voluntary involvement with social services, although increasing resource pressures and their effects on the ability of services to accept non-statutory work could make it more necessary to resort to court.

An example of the sort of case which may come under this paragraph was one which involved a severely disturbed twelve-year-old boy who had violently assaulted his parents, siblings, teachers and fellow pupils on a number of occasions over a period of some years. He had been received into care voluntarily in the past but his parents were reluctant to be seen to be putting him away and had requested his return. Eventually, it was agreed between his parents and social services that he should be the subject of care proceedings and that the onus for his removal to a residential school should lie with the department. Theoretically, the case might have been brought under the offence condition, but this seemed less stigmatizing. If one looks at the age and sex distribution of applications, one might also surmise that this ground is used for teenage runaways, again possibly as a less stigmatizing procedure than the moral danger or offence conditions. The word 'parent' is not specifically defined but court decisions have established that it includes adoptive parents and the natural mother, but not the father, of an illegitimate child.

Parents cannot bring proceedings on this ground themselves, but only by serving a written notice on the local authority requesting that they act. If the local authority does not commence proceedings within twenty-eight days, parents may ask the juvenile court to issue a direction to the authority (Children and Young Persons Act 1963 s. 3).

(e) he is of compulsory school age within the meaning of the Education Act 1944, and is not receiving efficient full-time education suitable to his age, ability and aptitude;

This is a counterpart to the powers available to local education authorities, under the Education Act 1944, to prosecute parents for failing to send their children to school. By bringing care proceedings under this subsection, education authorities may obtain orders which, in effect, can be used to compel children to attend. As such, this subsection is most commonly applied in cases of adolescent truancy, for children who are sent to school but fail to appear, where parental prosecution would seem inappropriate.

In fact, however, the scope of the clause is rather wider than this. Subsection 2(8)(b) of the 1969 Act defines how it may be satisfied. Firstly, the authority must prove that the child is of compulsory school age, that is to say, has reached the age of five and not reached the age of sixteen. In parental prosecution, the onus is on parents to prove that the child is not of school age, but this does not apply in care proceedings. Secondly, the authority must show that one of three further circumstances applies. The first of these is that the child is failing to comply with a school attendance order under section 37 of the Education Act 1944. Under this section, an education authority can require a parent to prove that his or her child is receiving suitable full-time education. If the authority is not satisfied, it can issue an order requiring the child to attend a named school. Failure to do so may lead either to the prosecution of the parent under section 40 of the 1944 Act, or to care proceedings against the child.

The second circumstance is that the child is failing to attend regularly at the school where he or she is registered. Section 39 of the 1944 Act defines non-attendance as an offence, unless it is due to sickness or 'any unavoidable cause', religious observance or the failure of the education authority to provide transport, where the child lives beyond the statutory walking distance from school. For children under eight, this is two miles by the most direct route, rising to three miles for older children. If the child's parents do not have a fixed address, this last does not apply but the parents must ensure that the child attends as regularly as possible and, in any event, at least 200 times in twelve months. Under the final circumstance envisaged by subsection 2(8)(b) of the 1969 Act, however, habitual vagrancy by the child's parent or adult caretaker can in itself be sufficient for an order to be made in care proceedings. In all of these cases, attendance is proved simply by the submission of a certificate from the headmaster of the relevant school stating the number of occasions on which the child was actually present at the time a register was taken.

This condition, then, can take in children whose parents have some conscientious objection to compulsory schooling and children of itinerant workers as well as the more straightforward truant. On the whole the courts have tended to take a very restrictive view of admissible objections to schooling. The burden of proof is on the child to show that the education he or she is receiving is as suitable as that offered by the education authority. In the nature of things this is a difficult test to meet because home tuition inevitably lacks the specialized facilities and social experiences even relatively poor schools can offer. Parental objections to particular forms of school organization, such as comprehensive as opposed to selective systems or mixed as opposed to single-sex provision, have generally been rejected as grounds for keeping children at home.

With children of itinerant workers we approach an area where education and welfare concerns merge. Although only education authorities may bring proceedings on this ground, there may be occasions on which the ease of proof can be used to seek care orders on children whose care is giving cause for anxiety. In such cases, discussion between social services and education welfare officers may lead to a decision to move under this condition, where the substantive concern can have more to do with the children's health or development. This can also be useful in some cases where there may be grounds for avoiding discussion of certain issues. What we have in mind here is a case of relatively young children living with their mother, who was psychiatrically disturbed to a degree that threatened the children's safety. Rather than expose her to further damage by making her conduct the central issue in proceedings on the proper development ground, social services and education agreed to proceed on the basis of the children's irregular school attendance.

The commonest type of proceedings, however, are fairly straightforward matters of truancy. Sixty per cent of all proceedings under this section are on fourteen- to seventeen-year-olds and a further thirty-five per cent on ten- to fourteen-year-olds. In describing truancy as 'straightforward', of course, we are begging important questions. How far should unwilling children be coerced into poor schools or, more precisely, perhaps, schools offering an education which they see as unattractive and irrelevant? This is an issue which we cannot discuss here but one which should concern magistrates, education and social services staff in areas with high truancy rates. It is also necessary to consider the administrative definition of truancy by education departments. Where do they draw the line? In some areas, fifty per cent attendance is defined as regular. In others, it is necessary to be absent for more than six consecutive weeks before any inquiry is made. A considerable length of time can elapse, and a good deal of schooling lost, before any action is taken. Even this is likely to be quite drawn out. Certainly it is a common complaint from magistrates that they always seem to be asked for care orders under this section on fifteen-and-a-half-year-olds.

(f) he is guilty of an offence, excluding homicide;

When this Act was originally passed, the then Labour government intended that ultimately all offenders under the age of fourteen would be dealt with by civil proceedings on this ground and would cease to be subject to criminal prosecution. Before the Act came fully into effect, however, there was a change of government. The Conservatives were opposed to the abolition of criminal proceedings for children and brought in, by the Criminal Justice Act 1972, a number of amendments to the 1969 Act which retained criminal prosecutions, although still leaving civil proceedings as an option. In criminal proceedings, it is only necessary to prove that the offence has occurred, rather than also having to prove a need for care or control, as we discuss below. Section 1 of the Guardianship of Minors Act 1971 obliges the magistrates to consider the child's interests as paramount in civil proceedings. By contrast, criminal proceedings are conducted with reference to the Children and Young Persons Act 1933, s. 44, which merely directs the magistrates to 'have regard' to the child's welfare. This permits a somewhat more punitive approach to juvenile criminals. One should not make too much of this contrast: as we see in subsequent chapters, civil care proceedings for offences have to follow special procedural rules which make them more like criminal proceedings than might be supposed. Nevertheless, the retreat from the welfare principles embodied in the original version of the 1969 Act has meant that only a handful of civil proceedings are initiated on the offence. In 1978, more than five and a half thousand care orders were made in criminal proceedings and just seven in civil proceedings under this paragraph.

This reversal of policy has had unfortunate consequences.

The procedure which care cases follow was designed on the assumption that children who had committed an offence would constitute a large proportion of the cases dealt with. In consequence, the form of the hearing is still quasi-criminal, with the child appearing, in effect, as a defendant, which makes for certain oddities in cases which are largely directed to the child's welfare. We shall discuss these at more length in a later chapter.

Nevertheless, it does seem unfortunate that this condition is so little used. One would have hoped that where police/social services liaison worked effectively, there might have been some attempt to analyse the circumstances which had led to the commission of an offence and to determine whether civil proceedings might be a more appropriate and less damaging course in the case of a particular child.

This ground cannot be used for children under ten, who are legally incapable of committing an offence. If they are found engaging in conduct which would constitute an offence for an older child, the most useful course might well lie under the moral danger provisions of subsection (c).

> and that he is in need of care or control which he is unlikely to receive unless the court makes an order under this section in respect of him, then, subject to the provisions of this section and sections 2 and 3 of this Act, the court may, if it thinks fit make such an order.

Very few court hearings actually seem to address this point as a separate issue. It often seems to be assumed that establishing the primary condition will be sufficient to pass this second test. On the other hand, we could see this as a reiteration of section 1 of the 1980 Act, that the court should be satisfied that everything appropriate has been done to achieve care or control without an order and has failed. An order is a last resort. Usually, of course, there will be ample evidence of the failure or irrelevance of voluntary intervention.

The 1969 Act is most appropriately used in cases where there is a history of failed voluntary intervention, with either parents or children, which has not led to any appreciable change in the children's circumstances or conduct or where there is such a substantial risk to the child's future wellbeing that his or her safety and interests can only be protected by removal into care with a degree of security. In conjunction with place of safety orders, care proceedings have great advantages as a basis for emergency intervention but there are limitations on their application and considerable procedural difficulties, especially for parents. Where the option exists, parents will almost always be in a more satisfactory legal position following a Section 3 resolution, under the 1980 Act, but this, of course, can only be passed if the child has come into care voluntarily.

This chapter has described the grounds on which care proceedings may be brought and given some examples of their scope and limitations. If used creatively, the statute offers a generous view of circumstances where children might require care or protection, although these are, again, subject to the overriding objective in the 1980 Act of preventing the need for proceedings. These circumstances should also acquire a degree of legitimacy from their status as explicitly approved legislative statements, rather than the subjective creation of judges. Nevertheless, there are many procedural complexities, particularly in relation to the part afforded to parents.

Chapter 5

Beginning Care Proceedings

On 20th May the social worker saw the medical clinical assistant in charge of the Maternity Unit to discuss the family and to explain the [Place of Safety] Order. She visited the hospital on both 20th and 21st May and spoke to the nursing staff on duty about the Order. A copy of the Order was left at the Hospital and was filed in the case notes but it is not clear when or by whom. As a result of these communications the social worker felt assured that the medical and nursing staff understood its implications . . . On Saturday 22nd May, mother and baby were certified by the medical clinical assistant as fit for discharge and they left the hospital that afternoon.

Simon Peacock Inquiry   1978

The grounds set out in section 1(2) of the Children and Young Persons Act 1969 gives a general indication of the circumstances in which compulsory measures of intervention may be appropriate. If a fieldworker in any agency is dealing with such a case and concludes that voluntary intervention has failed, legal action may be initiated. This chapter looks at the first steps in that process. We shall concentrate initially on protective intervention under grounds (a) – (d), reserving education and criminal matters for separate discussion at the end.

Legal Advice

A constant theme of this book is the necessary interdependence of people in a variety of agencies concerned with the care or protection of children. While most initial identifications of children's problems are made outside local authority social services departments, it is these which control most of the significant resources for voluntary intervention and which have, *de facto*, a near-monopoly on the right to initiate proceedings if compulsory measures are required. Conversely, if proceedings are necessary, the social services are likely to be heavily dependent upon the evidence of other agencies. It is, therefore, vitally important to ensure that adequate consultation takes place before embarking on legal action, that all agencies are committed to it and that they will honour this commitment throughout. This is one of the functions usually served by a case conference.

What is often overlooked, however, is the importance of legal advice at this stage. If there is any question of a need for compulsory measures, then it is essential that the case conference members should feel reasonably confident of obtaining the desired order. Otherwise they risk the withdrawal of voluntary cooperation by parents and may find themselves both anxious and impotent. Adequate legal advice may prevent such false starts. Conversely, case conference participants may fail to realize the strength of their own evidence. This is a point to which we shall return in chapter 8, but many fieldworkers have an unrealistic view of the stringency of legal rules and the scope of admissible material. In the absence of sound advice a case conference may wrongly conclude that its case is too weak to present. Finally, where there is great concern but weak evidence, a legal adviser may be able to suggest what would be needed to strengthen the case, or could explore alternative legal measures.

The appropriate place to look for legal advice is the legal department of the local authority. Unfortunately, these vary a good deal in the interest and status afforded to child care work. What should be remembered is that career advancement for solicitors in local government is related much more to their involvement with committees and councillors than to the sort of advocacy involved in child care. In some authorities, care cases are dealt with at arm's length. Much of the preliminary work

may be done by a courts section in the social services department and the solicitor only becomes involved at the door of the
court. In these circumstances, the courts section may acquire a
good deal of ad hoc legal expertise. Nevertheless, this is usually
less satisfactory than the knowledge and training which a lawyer
can bring to bear. Many authorities have considerably enlarged
the scope of legal involvement so that a lawyer is, in principle,
available to attend every case conference. This seems to be
much more desirable from all points of view – children, parents,
staff and courts – as a way of ensuring that cases are properly
based in law and presented in a coherent fashion. The increased
contact is instructive for both health and social service workers
and for the solicitors themselves. One cannot, though, escape
the basic problem that there is a high turnover of rather young
and inexperienced solicitors. Other agencies do have to be
prepared to accommodate this constant change and the associated process of learning as new solicitors are inducted and
acquire the understanding of health and social welfare services
needed to represent them effectively.

In some places, other agencies, especially health authorities,
like their employees to consult the agency's own legal advisers at
some stage if there is any question of becoming involved in
proceedings. These advisers are usually partners in large private
practices. On the whole, this process is a waste of both time and
money. Child care law is a specialized area which is seldom
encountered in private practice, especially by senior members
of large firms. If there is a problem, it is much more appropriate
to go to the relevant local authority solicitor. These lawyers
should not be seen as somehow in the pocket of social services.
Their obligations lie firstly to the court and secondly to the local
authority as a whole, rather than to any particular client department. If, say, giving evidence on a particular point is likely to
cause problems for somebody working in another agency, it will
almost always be better to make a direct approach to the solicitor
handling the case. He can then appraise its significance for his
presentation in court and discuss ways of circumventing the
problem. A health visitor following up a neighbour's tip-off
about a child's treatment, for instance, may be worried about

disclosing the reason for visiting on a particular day. If the local authority's solicitor knows this, he can avoid the point in his own questions and be ready to head the matter off, should it be raised in cross-examination. Most local authority solicitors do not subscribe to a 'hired-gun' view of their role as an advocate. They would regard it as quite reasonable to be asked for impartial advice by potential witnesses from other agencies, even at some cost to their own case.

So we argue that where a case has been of concern for some time and people are gradually moving towards a decision to intervene, then expert legal advice should have been made available, in some form or other, during the discussions and certainly at case conferences where crucial decisions may be taken. Similarly, if the case has arisen suddenly by, for example the admission of a child to hospital with suspicious injuries and a case conference is called while the doctors are keeping the child in for observation, efforts should be made to ensure that expert legal advice is available at that conference. But there are occasions where a fieldworker may need to act without having had the opportunity to receive such advice. These would be emergencies when there is reason to believe that a child is in immediate danger of injury or further injury by remaining in his or her present location or by being removed from present secure surroundings. The means for taking this emergency action is primarily the place of safety order. In such a case it would be unusual to expect the fieldworker to take expert legal advice before acting, although consultation with a senior colleague would be normal.

Place of Safety Orders

Section 28 of the Children and Young Persons Act 1969 lays down two ways in which a child may come to be detained in a place of safety. The first of these, which is available to *any* citizen, is on application to a magistrate for a place of safety order. This *may* (not must) be granted if the magistrate is satisfied that the applicant has 'reasonable cause to believe' that any of the conditions (a) – (e), for making a care order discussed in chapter 4 are satisfied, or (in the case of grounds (b) and (bb)) would be found by an appropriate court. If granted, the order authorizes the detention of the child in a place of safety for twenty-eight days, or a specified shorter period. This provision offers obvious possibilities to anyone faced with a recalcitrant social services department. On the other hand, such independent action is unlikely to promote good relations between agencies and should be contemplated only as a last resort with support at the highest level. More realistically, health service personnel could find it useful where there are problems in emergency contact with social services out of hours or in sparsely populated rural areas. Here, though, one might expect some prior agreement at a case conference, or at least in a telephone conversation, even if the actual dealings with the magistrate were not by a social worker. The other method is available only to the police. A constable may himself physically detain a child in a place of safety if he has reasonable cause to believe that the same conditions are met, but he must 'as soon as possible' refer the matter to a senior police officer who must then either release the child or may authorize his or her continued detention for a period up to eight days.

The local authority social services are required to receive and maintain a child on a place of safety order (Child Care Act 1980, s. 73(1)(a)). However, the order remains in force to the applicant so, if this is not a local authority employee, the child's placement must be managed in consultation with the person named on the order.

A number of important points should be noted about these provisions. Firstly, they do not permit anyone to enter property against the will of the occupants and to remove a child by force. The fieldworker will have to rely on acquiring voluntary entry or the fact that the child is already out of the home (perhaps temporarily in residential care or hospital). If forcible entry is required, then the police must be involved and a warrant for entry obtained from a magistrate under section 40 of the Children and Young Persons Act 1933. This section allows a magistrate to issue, to anyone applying in the interests of the child, a warrant authorizing a constable to search for and remove a child where there is reasonable cause to believe that the child is being or has been assaulted, ill-treated or neglected or with respect to whom certain offences are being or have been committed. The same procedure holds good if a child already in care has been abducted by the parents and the authorities wish to retrieve him or her from private premises.

Secondly, in some districts, an arrangement has been made that applications for place of safety orders must be channelled through a clerk of the magistrates' court before being passed on to a magistrate. This is an entirely administrative procedure, with no basis in statute, but it does mean that applications are reviewed for their basic soundness by someone with a legal qualification. Social services departments and emergency services should ensure, if such an arrangement exists, that information about any rota system operating among the clerks is easily accessible. While no clerk would have the right to refuse to forward an application to a magistrate, it is possible that he might encourage the magistrate to scrutinize the application closely. Nor should it be assumed that the applicant is in any way 'entitled' to an order authorizing the child's detention for the full twenty-eight-day period. Some magistrates (perhaps under the influence of the clerks) may want the case to be brought before the juvenile court as soon as possible, possibly at its next sitting (which may be within the week). If this is so, the matter should swiftly be put into the hands of the legal department so that an application can be made to the court for an interim care order (see below).

It should be remembered that, as we discussed in chapter 4, a care order cannot, except in restricted circumstances, be made where the only basis is fear of injury to the child in the future. It follows that a place of safety order cannot be made either in such a case. This limitation could cause an acute dilemma for field-workers who are fearful that a child might suffer serious injury or death unless something is immediately done. In such a case it is probable that a magistrate would not rely on what would be considered a 'technicality' and the order would be granted. Alternatively an eight-day detention by the police could be sought, as they are more likely to be moved to action out of concern for the child than deterred by legal niceties. The technical question would then be left to arise at the care proceedings themselves, always assuming it is raised by somebody. By that stage, too, the lawyers will have been able to consider whether they would wish to circumvent the whole problem by using wardship proceedings.

Place of safety orders do no more than authorize the detention of the child, and give no further rights. This fact is not widely appreciated and its implications are a little uncertain. It is doubtful whether parents can be required to contribute financially to the child's maintenance. Most importantly, the authorities probably do not acquire the right to carry out medical or psychiatric assessments of the child (except insofar as they may be necessary to safeguard the child's immediate health) unless the parents consent. Some assessment centres appreciate this point and will normally wait until an interim care order has been obtained before proceeding to such assessments, although even here the legal basis is uncertain. The point is less likely to be appreciated by medical personnel. However, parents could be made aware that failure to cooperate is likely to show them up in a bad light when the case eventually comes before the juvenile court.

Finally, although the statute is silent on the point, it is very unlikely that it would be proper to apply for a second place of safety order when the first one expires, thus in effect obtaining an extension of the time initially granted.

How to Proceed after a Place of Safety Order

Care proceedings need not necessarily be preceded by a place of safety order, but it is usually wise to obtain one: if this is not done and the parents ask for the child back at any time before the hearing, the child has to be returned to them. On the other hand, it should not be thought that care proceedings must necessarily follow the obtaining of a place of safety order. Agency personnel must ask themselves what they hope to achieve by bringing care proceedings. It is sometimes thought that the mere fact that proceedings have been brought will be enough to 'bring the parents to their senses' and modify their behaviour towards their children. It is possible that this might also be a correct assessment of the effects of having taken a place of safety order.

Other legal avenues besides care proceedings might also be relevant. If, as is often the case, the origin of the threat to the children lies in marital discord between the adults, the solution may lie in the institution by one of the parents of divorce or other matrimonial proceedings. In particular, the power of magistrates' courts or a county court to make an order excluding from the home an adult whose behaviour is threatening the safety of the other adult or any children should be considered a possible option. The power of the county courts extends to making exclusion orders against an adult occupier whether or not the adults are married, and it does not matter who owns or rents the property. Proceedings of this kind must, of course, be brought by one of the parties concerned; there is no power for the local authority to institute them. But they may be the most appropriate route to a lasting solution and could effect a rapid return home for the children. It is not the function of this book to describe the details of such proceedings, but fieldworkers should be aware of their existence and prepared to obtain legal advice about them where it seems appropriate. The local authority lawyer involved in the case may raise the point himself, but even if he does not, there is no reason why a fieldworker should not suggest that these possibilities be explored.

The advisability of pursuing care proceedings will depend very much on what the authority wishes to obtain from them. Here it is necessary to consider briefly what orders the court can make if the grounds are found proved. (These are examined more fully in chapter 9.) It can order the parents to enter into recognizances with respect to their future behaviour. This is like being bound over in criminal proceedings: the parents agree to take some specified action for a particular period. If they fail, then an agreed fine will automatically be imposed. This option is little used except in truancy cases, but may be appropriate if it is felt that the parents will respond to the 'fright' of being brought before a court. But the most usual options are the care order and the supervision order. The former transfers all powers and responsibilities regarding the child to the local authority; the latter simply puts the authority under a duty to 'advise, assist and befriend' the supervised person, who is the child concerned.

Apart from the possibility (little used) that a court may make it a condition that the supervised person shall be medically examined in accordance with arrangements made by the supervisor, the supervision order provides no opportunity to issue binding directions regarding the care of the child. Nor does the possession of the order give the supervisor (who would usually be a local authority social worker) the power to enter premises or remove or detain the child. Its only real advantage is that, once it has been obtained, the local authority may return to court at a later stage and seek for its conversion into a care order without having to prove the primary grounds again. Social services departments rarely see much point in supervision orders for child protection cases. These orders impose a duty on them with no corresponding powers. An order can jeopardize voluntary casework with parents and gives no additional leverage for securing their cooperation. As we shall see, courts sometimes make supervision orders in cases where they think the evidence is rather marginal, as a supposed 'soft option'. Where child protection is concerned, the result is an illusion of action, responsibility without authority.

In most cases, then, the advantage of a care order will impel the local authority towards that option. Although the basic concern may still be for the child's immediate safety, however, the presentation of the application in court will require some view to be taken of the child's longer-term future. The transfer of parental powers to the local authority is complete and the child's management under a care order is at the authority's discretion. Although magistrates may sometimes appear to do so, the court cannot instruct the authority on the use of its discretion. Any such comments from the Bench can safely be disregarded. However, before deciding what order to make, the court is likely to be faced with questions about the authority's plans for the child, which may well influence the choice, for example, between a care or a supervison order. It is obviously prudent for the authority to anticipate this and to have a reasonably coherent plan for the child to set out at the hearing. Care orders confer a great deal of power on a local authority, and it seems inappropriate for them to be made where the authority is uncertain of its own objectives in using that power.

At the same time, the wide discretion inherent in a care order gives the authority considerable flexibility in attempting to protect a child. An order can be used to achieve a complete and final break between parents and child. Equally, the authority can work towards the rehabilitation of the child in the family, perhaps after therapy for the whole family unit (or at least mother and children) outside the home, or after giving the adult(s) time and help to overcome the problems which led to the threat to the child. On the other hand, it may not be thought that the child should be removed from the home at all, or, if so, not for more than a very short time. The object might be to try to overcome the difficulties without breaking up the family but to create conditions which give the authority the maximum opportunity both to exercise surveillance over the family and to put pressure on the adults to modify their behaviour.

This last point demands special comment. Some people think that, if an authority obtains a care order, it is improper to plan to keep the child at home. It is a view that some lawyers take, and may even be adopted by some social workers. The reasons for this are very mixed. Sometimes it seems to rest on the idea that when the court makes a care order it does so on the assumption that the child will be removed from home, and that to seek a care order while intending all along not to remove the child is in some way to deceive the court. It may indeed be true that where magistrates make a care order with respect to children they have convicted of offences, they expect them to be removed from home. But there is no reason to believe that they necessarily expect this to happen in a child care case. Furthermore, section 21(2) of the Child Care Act 1980 expressly permits the authority to allow a child in its care to be under the charge and control of a parent, guardian, relative or friend for a fixed period or until the authority otherwise determines.

It may also be thought that to allow a child home who has been committed into the care of the local authority could create a confusion in the minds of both social workers and parents as to how responsibility for the child is divided between them. This could happen, of course, but may be avoided by careful explanation to all concerned about where true responsibility lies. The advantage, in some cases, of adopting this procedure is that, without undergoing the trauma of removing the child totally from home, the authority acquires under the care order the power at any time physically to remove the child without having to return to court (although a fieldworker could not enter premises without a warrant: see above p. 69). In this way the local authority can 'bargain' with the parents from a position of considerable power. The practice holds its risks, both for the authority (if things go wrong) and the parents (because it potentially subjects them to a very wide measure of pressure from the authority). For this reason, it should only be adopted after careful consideration. At the same time, it is of the essence of a care order that such a discretion exists, if the child's interests seem best served by this course of action.

Involvement of the Police

Police involvement may emerge as a significant complicating factor while plans are being made for a child held on a place of safety order. This might already have happened in extreme cases at the outset in order to secure the child's immediate safety. In other cases the police may have been introduced onto the scene because it is standard procedure to notify them of case conferences dealing with children who have been the subject of injuries or neglect, either of which may constitute a ground for the criminal prosecution of adults.

It is important to clarify the role of the police in child abuse and neglect cases. In the first place, a social worker or other member of a child protection agency is under no duty, any more than any other citizen, to inform the police of offences he or she may get to know about. So long as the worker does not receive money to be silent, or mislead the police in their inquiries, such information need not be passed on. However, the police have an independent right, which they may exercise on their own initiative, both to institute care proceedings on any ground except that of truancy and to prosecute people for any criminal offences that may have been committed. The first power is rarely exercised. It could put the social services department in a very difficult position because, should the police succeed and obtain a care or supervision order, the child becomes the responsibility of the department. However, if the police have come to know about a case of abuse or neglect, the possibility that they might exercise that power, or threaten to use it, if the local authority does not take action, cannot be dismissed.

The power to prosecute for offences in connection with the case causes many more problems. These derive mainly from two issues. In the first place, many lawyers think that, if an adult is to be prosecuted for an offence against the child, the hearing of the care proceedings should only take place after the trial of the adult. Their reason is that it is regarded as a fundamental principle that an accused person should not be obliged to disclose to the police the nature of his defence before the trial. If the care proceedings took place before the trial the adults would probably wish to 'disclose their defence' at those proceedings, and this would be public knowledge, or at least, might come to the attention of the prosecution. If this reasoning is followed, the hearing of the care proceedings could be greatly delayed. This causes considerable difficulties for social workers because their long-term plans for a child might depend upon the outcome of the criminal proceedings; for example, it might be relevant to know whether a parent will be in prison.

This is an issue on which opinions can reasonably differ. It is our view that the fear of premature disclosures is exaggerated. The reason why accused people need not disclose their defence to the police before trial is to protect them against police pressure. If the police happen to find out, indirectly, what excuses someone intends to offer at their trial, no one can complain of unfairness. This seems to cover the situation where care proceedings precede a criminal prosecution. Where the postponement of care proceedings while waiting for a criminal trial would cause serious difficulties in planning for the child, we would certainly argue that the care proceedings should go ahead.

Social workers must be careful not to allow their judgement about the propriety of bringing care proceedings to be influenced by what happens concerning criminal proceedings. For example, the mere fact that the police decide not to prosecute should not deter the authority from initiating care proceedings. Similarly, the result of a prosecution (whether conviction or acquittal) should not in itself determine the matter. The specific issues before the criminal court, its procedures and rules of evidence may be very different from those which would be relevant in care proceedings.

Relations between the police and social workers in cases of child abuse and neglect can very frequently give rise to tension and misunderstanding. This of course flows from the very different orientations of the two professions and to some extent from a genuine uncertainty in the public mind as to what the true role of the criminal law should be in these cases. The police, quite properly from their point of view, will insist on their right to prosecute people who commit criminal offences against children and thus to 'vindicate the law'. On the other hand, many senior policemen have stated that they are fully aware of the complexities of violence which occurs in domestic settings and claim that their response will fully take into account the effects of prosecution on the whole family.

The success of the balance which is struck between the concerns of fieldworkers and those of the police will depend largely on the personal relationships and formal channels of communication between social welfare agencies and the police in different areas. One common problem seems to be that social services are kept in the dark, sometimes for quite long periods, while the police consider their decision whether to prosecute, or, if so, what offences to charge a person with. It would seem desirable that communication between the two agencies is maintained during this period. At the same time, social workers must recognize their own contribution to some of these difficulties. If they consistently attempt to shut the police out, they cannot reasonably complain if they do not receive full cooperation or if uninformed police officers act in an insensitive fashion.

One area where collaboration between the police and social services can be fruitful is in investigation. In cases where a child has been injured but it is not clear which adult is responsible, the police may be able to find the culprit more easily than a social worker could. Indeed, social workers may prefer that the police conduct the kind of investigation that may be needed in order to find the true facts. Similarly, the access that the police have to criminal records can be very useful in ascertaining whether, for example, an adult member of a household has previous convictions for violence. But against this, the police have sometimes been accused of insensitivity in the conduct of inquiries, perhaps where the case has sexual implications, or in relatively minor cases where they may send a uniformed officer round to a parent's place of work. Some of these difficulties might be avoided if social services personnel and the police discussed cases together more fully and were able more frequently to coordinate their actions.

Offence and Education Proceedings

These two types of proceeding may usefully be looked at together, as they are both based on the notion of an offence or quasi-offence being committed by the child. As we have observed, the police have an independent right to bring civil care proceedings on any ground, other than truancy. Social services departments, but not the NSPCC, may use the offence condition. Truancy proceedings are the exclusive prerogative of education departments in local authorities.

We have already discussed the reluctance of either police or social services to use the offence condition. Most proceedings relating to offending juveniles, then, come under section 7(7) of the Children and Young Persons Act 1969. This allows courts to make care or supervision orders or orders requiring a parent to enter into a recognizance, as a result of criminal proceedings in the juvenile court. No child under ten may be prosecuted and those aged between ten and fourteen must be shown to know right from wrong before a case can proceed. The prosecutor must notify the local authority, and for a child over thirteen, the probation service, before proceedings may begin. In theory, this should allow for consultation on the child's welfare, but areas vary widely in the diligence with which this is undertaken.

Only education departments may bring truancy proceedings. Since these can result in the child being committed to the care of the social services, a degree of advance interdepartmental liaison is obviously valuable, although not required by statute. In this situation, proceedings will need to establish that the child is either failing to comply with a school attendance order or to attend regularly without an adequate reason, as specified in section 39 of the Education Act 1944, or is the child of an itinerant worker and has failed to attend at least 200 times in twelve months.

Both of these types of proceeding are more likely to follow the issue of a notice than a place of safety order. This procedure may also be more appropriate in certain other cases where the emergency detention of a child seems unnecessary. The issue of notices is a technical matter which will be carried out by the social services department's courts section or the authority's legal department. Fieldworkers need not be concerned over the details of procedure.

Interim Orders

If the local authority is not ready to proceed with the hearing of care proceedings by the time a place of safety order expires, the child will have to be returned to his or her parents unless they agree voluntarily to leave him or her in care. As we have seen, the maximum period under which a child can be held on a place of safety order is twenty-eight days, and even this may sometimes be restricted. The local authority's lawyers will therefore be under some pressure to prepare their case. If they are not ready, they may nevertheless ask the juvenile court for an interim care order which transfers parental rights to the local authority, but which only lasts for twenty-eight days. However, at the end of that period a further application may be made, and indeed there is no limit to the number of interim orders that may be granted. This frequently happens if the local authority is waiting for criminal proceedings to be brought against an adult in connection with the child.

There is, however, a certain tendency to regard applications for interim orders as a mere formality which will always be granted (unless the matter has become intolerably drawn out) and to which the 'other side' will take no objection. But strictly an interim order should not be made unless the court is satisfied that the primary grounds discussed in chapter 4 are satisfied with respect to the child. The device is simply intended to allow the court time to consider what the best order would be. Sometimes the lawyers representing other parties may take this point, so the authority should always be ready to be able to make out its case in the event of opposition. In practice, however, unless criminal proceedings are pending, the local authority is usually in a position to go ahead within twenty-eight days. Applications for interim orders often seem to be made by agreement because the other lawyers are not yet ready to proceed. As we shall explain in chapter 7, there are reasons why these lawyers have difficulty in preparing their case as quickly as might be thought desirable.

These delays can be very frustrating to social workers. They can also cause resentment to other people who may be involved. To come to court in the belief that there may be a hearing only to be sent away again because everyone has agreed to an interim order being granted can be very annoying. It would usually be wise to require the lawyers to make it very clear in advance whether or not there is likely to be a full hearing before putting a lot of people to great inconvenience.

This chapter has stressed the need for appropriate specialist legal advice from an early stage in child protection matters. In an emergency, it will, however, usually be necessary for agency staff to act independently to obtain a place of safety order. Anyone can apply to a magistrate for such an order and we have described its scope and limitations. Once a child has come into care in this fashion, legal involvement is essential in shaping responsible plans for a child's future. If compulsory measures are necessary, these may entail one or more applications for interim care orders.

Chapter 6

The Court Hearing

We have given some thought to the suggestion made in several quarters that the Magistrates Court is not the appropriate forum for discussions about the future and safety of children. In particular it has been said that a decision of this kind is a social rather than a legal one and that the traditional system for deciding disputes between two parties is 'neither helpful nor appropriate in determining where the interests of a child at risk may lie' (letter to 'The Times', 2nd November, 1976). . . At the same time we can see that polarisation of the issues is perhaps necessary and inevitable when the liberty of the individual is at stake. In such cases the evidence ought to be tested rigorously to establish the right and proper basis of fact, on which grave decisions affecting children are to be made. The present method has the merits and safeguards built into centuries of judicial practice. As to whether it is flexible enough to be adapted to the adjudication of issues such as these, we are in two minds.

Wayne Brewer Inquiry   1977

Care proceedings are heard in magistrates' courts. This means, outside London and one or two other metropolitan centres, that matters are decided by a panel of part-time lay magistrates who are advised on legal questions by a permanent official, the court clerk. The atmosphere of the court, its procedures and the ways in which statutes and regulations are interpreted rest on a fine balance between legality and common sense, the restraints of law and the practical conceptions of justice developed by ordinary men and women. The next three chapters examine court hearings in some detail, since they are the least understood and probably the most stressful part of the whole experience of coercive action for both agency staff and families. This chapter provides an overview of the basic nature of the hearings and their procedural structure. In the following chapters, two particularly troublesome issues – representation and evidence – will receive more extended discussion.

The Nature of the Hearing

Although care proceedings take place in magistrates' courts, it is essential to recognize that they are not criminal proceedings. Even if the grounds are found to be proven, this does not constitute a conviction of either the parents or the child. Indeed, all parties may be wholly free of any moral blame.

Unfortunately, it is easy for the civil nature of these matters to be lost in a welter of minor details. The court buildings will regularly be handling large numbers of criminal cases and inevitably be associated with such work. Uniformed policemen unconnected with the case are almost certain to be in evidence around the building and even sometimes in the courtroom itself. This latter is quite unnecessary in most cases, and magistrates might reasonably be asked to ensure that it does not happen. Although the case may be heard on a day or in a courtroom specifically designated for juvenile work, most of this concerns young offenders. About 148,000 young people were dealt with in criminal proceedings in 1978 as against 6,000 or so in care proceedings. People connected with child protection cases may have to wait side by side with those who have come to court on straightforward criminal charges.

Secondly, the fact that the application is made by a public body inevitably leads people to draw parallels with police prosecutions. Even magistrates can be misled into thinking of the local authority as the 'prosecution' or, worse still, referring to them as such. If this happens, the matter should be pursued at the highest level, probably through the Area Review Committee, to ensure that magistrates are fully sensitive to the nature of these cases. Finally, the evidence which is given will often appear to be attacking the character of a child's parents. If the parents are legally represented, their lawyers may add to this impression by adopting techniques and attitudes more reminiscent of defending lawyers in a criminal case.

Yet these are indeed civil proceedings, a fact which is of fundamental importance in understanding the procedures which are followed, the evidence which is admissible and the standards of proof which are applied. Probably the most helpful way of looking at them is to imagine the case as one which is brought by a child against his or her parents, in the same way as a wife might bring an action against her husband for failing properly to provide for their family. The only difference is that, because of the child's age, the case has to be brought on his or her behalf by a third party, generally the local authority. The parents are not being punished so much as the child's rights are being secured. This formulation is somewhat less useful with older children being dealt with as quasi-delinquents on the grounds of moral danger, being beyond control, or truancy, but it is one of the inherent problems of the 1969 Act that issues related to the care or protection of children are confused with issues related to the control of children. The latter categories are more like criminal proceedings, and this is an important source of tension within the hearing procedures, as we shall demonstrate.

Nevertheless, the notion of care proceedings as an attempt to secure children's entitlements does provide a more positive basis for thinking about how a case is put together and presented. It explains the prominent role which allegations against the parents' character or competence are likely to play. This approach can also provide a more satisfactory basis for casework with a family through the experience of the proceedings and, simultaneously, allay some of the anxieties of social workers about their involvement with coercive rather than therapeutic actions.

All the grounds specified in section 1(2) of the 1969 Act, with the partial exception of the offence condition, make some reference to the present state of the child, so the application for an order will require some, more or less objective, evidence of the child's condition. This may come from several quarters. If one is dealing with the child protection grounds – (a), (b) and (bb) – the evidence will be on the child's physical, emotional or mental state. Usually, this will be given by one or more doctors, and possibly a psychologist, who are in effect presenting clinical reports stating that, on examination, particular signs and symptoms were found to be present. Equivalent evidence will be necessary in other circumstances, of moral danger, lack of control or truancy. It should, however, rarely be considered sufficient. Further evidence will be needed, usually from social workers or health visitors, to show how those clinical descriptions are to be interpreted. This is where an evaluation of the parents' conduct is likely to be so important.

It may help to consider a specific example. Despite the views of some doctors, it is rarely, if ever, possible to distinguish accidental from non-accidental injuries solely on clinical evidence. Signs and symptoms are not self-explanatory but must be fitted into a context which allows those involved to decide whether they are non-accidental or whether, indeed, they result from a freak accident. The way in which this is done outside the court is to build up a social context for the event in question. A history is assembled. The parents' accounts of the injuries are scrutinized. Are their deficiencies due to lack of detail, which might be remedied by further questions, to genuine ignorance, if they did not observe the event, or to deliberate deception? As part of this process, the parents' moral character is evaluated. Are they the sort of people who could be lying? Even if they are not lying, does the very occurrence of the injury imply a lack of care? Have the parents adequately respected the child's need for protection from various social, physical or environmental hazards?

For the local authority to persuade the court, they must take the magistrates through this reasoning process and convince them that the most plausible account of the circumstances in question has been produced. In the course of this, it will also be necessary to show that voluntary measures are inappropriate, that a court order is indeed necessary. This will usually be done by examining the record of relationships between agencies and the family to establish that the authority has made reasonable efforts which have failed for lack of cooperation from the parents, whether through principle, incompetence or bloody-mindedness. Again, the parents' character will often be a central issue.

Giving evidence on these matters can put a great strain on the relationship between fieldworker and client. In fact it is not possible either to avoid this dilemma or to blame it on the adversarial nature of the legal system. Such a confrontation is really at the heart of the whole process of challenging the parents' upbringing of their children. We do better to realize this than to conceal it. In this respect, health visitors and hospital medical staff are in a stronger position than social workers and (possibly) general practitioners because they can more easily characterize their role as oriented towards the child alone than to the family in general. But it is this perspective which the fieldworker should try to get across in court. The evidence may appear to be an attack on the parents. But if this is so, it is only true insofar as their conduct has a bearing on the child's welfare. This is why the present formal structure of proceedings is so unfortunate. Because it was assumed that most of the cases dealt with would result from the offence condition, the procedures derive from a model which presupposes a contest between the local authority and the child. For most purposes, though, care proceedings are not an occasion for punishing either children or their parents. If this is the objective, then the proper course is through criminal proceedings, although, of course, in the case of children many of the dispositions are formally the same.

Care proceedings are a way in which the child, through the local authority, is complaining about the quality of care which he or she is receiving and asking that the court make such provisions as will rectify this. What the authority's witnesses must get across is that the child does have this basic civil and legal right for his or her parents to be called to account for their conduct.

The Structure of the Court Hearing

Technically the proceedings are started by the authority 'bringing the child before the court'. In fact, unless the child is under five, in which case the authority may get dispensation, the child must literally be present throughout the proceedings. The magistrates, however, do have a discretion, under the Magistrates' Courts (Children and Young Persons) Rules 1970, to require the child to withdraw during the presentation of evidence, if they consider this to be in the child's interests. Most courts seem happy to stretch this to excuse children in abuse or neglect cases, but of course it is less appropriate for grounds like truancy or being beyond control, where there is indeed more obviously a case against the child.

In theory, the hearing should fall into two distinct stages: establishing the grounds and considering the order which will be appropriate. The first part will involve the applicant, almost invariably the local authority, in showing that one or more of the grounds set out in section 1(2) of the 1969 Act exists in respect of the child who is before the court. In order to do this, they will present written or, more usually, oral evidence from witnesses, which can then be tested in cross-examination. The evidence must satisfy the civil standard of proof, the balance of probabilities, rather than the criminal standard, beyond reasonable doubt, except where proceedings are being brought under the offence condition. It is difficult to define the practical difference between these tests. The civil standard is less stringent, in principle, since the court must only be satisfied that it is more likely than not that the applicant's allegations are true. On the other hand, in care proceedings the gravity of the allegations is often such that magistrates seem to put a rather conservative interpretation on this more elastic standard.

The parties to the hearing are the applicants and the child. As a party, the child will be entitled to legal aid and to take a full part in the hearing, calling his or her own witnesses and cross-examining the other party's. The child's parents are not parties, even though much of the evidence may relate to their conduct. This means that their participation is more restricted and subject to the court's discretion. Parents are not eligible for legal aid and their rights are limited to meeting allegations against them, by calling or giving evidence, and in certain circumstances to making representations to the court. In particular, they do not have a right to cross-examine either party's witnesses, although the court has a discretion to permit this. Few courts, in fact, seem prepared to rule out parents on this technicality. We shall come to these points at more length in the next chapter, but, once again, the influence of a criminal model on the people who drafted the 1969 Act should be apparent. If it is assumed that most cases will arise from juvenile delinquency or very similar conduct, this arrangement makes sense. Since the majority of cases are based on the protection grounds, the statuses of both parents and children are rather at odds with the nature of the issues involved.

Typically, the hearing will begin by the local authority's lawyer outlining the case to be presented. This will be followed by evidence supporting the application. The authority's lawyer will take each witness through his or her evidence, what is called the examination-in-chief. Once he has finished with each witness, they may be cross-examined, firstly by the child's lawyer and then, if the court permits, by the parents or their lawyer. The witness may be re-examined by the authority's lawyer. Once the applicant's case has been set out, the child's lawyer can address the court. He may invite the magistrates to find that the case has not been made out, in which case the bench will probably retire to consider whether there is, indeed, a case to answer. If there is, or if the lawyer does not want to take the technical point, he can outline the child's case and call witnesses on the child's behalf. He will conduct an examination-in-chief, followed by the authority's cross-examination, the parents' cross-examination, if permitted, and any further re-examination. Finally, the parents may call their own witnesses or give evidence on their own behalf, which is open to examination in the same way. We shall look at the content and presentation of evidence in more detail in chapter 8.

After the evidence is completed, either party may address the court again. For some reason local authority lawyers seldom seem to take up this option, a point which often baffles social workers and others, especially as the other lawyers generally do. It is hard to see why this opportunity is not used more often, and the courts might well find it helpful in focusing on the central issues.

This concludes the first part of the hearing, and the magistrates usually retire to consider whether the case has been proved. If they find it has not, the matter is dismissed. If the case has been made out, the proceedings go into a second stage where the court decides on the appropriate order. To help them in this, they will have a social inquiry or home surroundings report prepared by a social worker, describing the child's background, home circumstances and family history. The magistrates will read it, and copies will be shown to the child's solicitor and, at the court's discretion, to the parents or their solicitor. In practice, the child's solicitor or the court clerk will often take the parents aside and go through the report with them. The report's author will usually go into the witness box to answer any questions, whether from the magistrates, the parents or the child's solicitor, about its content or recommendations. The court will then decide what order to make. We shall look at the possible dispositions and at social inquiry reports in chapter 9.

One of the implications of this two-stage process is that matters which are relevant to the second stage should not be discussed in the first. It would be wrong, for instance, to go into the authority's plans for a child before the grounds had been proved. Moreover, there is a crucial difference in the rules of evidence. All information in the first stage must be established within the rules. Similar constraints do not apply to social inquiry reports, which may not be challenged on technical grounds such as their use of hearsay or opinion.

As so often in these proceedings, however, these firm theoretical distinctions become blurred in practice. Some courts maintain this separation very strongly, while others have effectively abandoned it. There is some justification for this in the 'care or control' part of section 1(2). It could be said that the need to establish what care or control is desirable, but is not

likely to be provided, implies discussion of the possible dispositions. However, it is rare for this issue to be separately considered. Most courts seem to assume that, where a primary
ground exists regarding a child, the need for 'care' (if not
'control') has been established. More importantly, the 'care or
control' test only asks that the court be satisfied at the first stage
that the child's proper care requires 'an' order to be made. This
will usually be implicitly dealt with in the authority's allegations
that it has tried to deal with the parents on a voluntary basis, but
has failed. It does not necessarily imply that there should be
consideration at this stage of the type of order that should be
made.

The danger of discussing disposition at the first stage is that it
can dissolve into a kind of 'plea bargaining'. By this we mean an
attempt to negotiate an agreement to refrain from contesting the
first part, if a lesser order, most commonly for supervision
rather than care, is made in the second. Anybody may initiate
this. If he has a weak case, the local authority lawyer may
announce in advance that he is only instructed to seek a supervision order in the hope that the court will be more ready to find
the case proved. Should this succeed, the authority can come
back to court and ask for the supervision order to be converted
to a care order without having to establish the grounds again.
Sometimes the magistrates prompt a discussion, perhaps in the
hope of encouraging a disposition which seems less punitive to
the parents. Most often, however, the parents initiate the
negotiation by promising future cooperation if only a
supervision order is sought. Because of the emotive nature of
the issues, some magistrates are inclined to be unduly
impressed by such parental protestations and to rely on
'undertakings' given by parents in court. Such undertakings
have no legal validity whatsoever and are quite unenforceable.
Moreover the whole point of bringing care proceedings is likely
to be that the parents have had a number of 'last chances' to
cooperate and failed.

While there is probably no real harm in the authority disclosing its general objectives, this sort of negotiation does seem
undesirable, at least in the first stage. But it is difficult to resist,

since magistrates are often reluctant to appear oppressive by ruling out questions on technical grounds. If it does come up, then local authority witnesses should stand by their assessments. When it has been decided after careful reflection and discussion that a child's interest cannot adequately be safeguarded, other than by means of a care order, the court is not the place to depart from that judgement. Indeed, it may be important to use such questions to underline the collapse of previous voluntary efforts at intervention. This sort of courtroom craft is a matter which we shall look at further in our discussions of evidence-giving.

Care proceedings are heard in magistrates' courts before lay justices. They are civil proceedings, not criminal prosecutions, and are heard according to civil rules of evidence with a civil standard of proof. Proceedings have two elements – the establishment of grounds and the decision on disposition – although these may be somewhat blurred in practice. Especially where the case relates to abuse or neglect, it is helpful to think of it as an action by the local authority, on behalf of the child, to secure the child's entitlement to a certain quality of care, and not as any action specifically against parents.

Chapter 7

Representation

At some point in her evidence Mrs Kepple was clearly asked the question – whether by her solicitor or the Court cannot be determined – what was Mr Kepple's attitude to Maria, because her answer is recorded by the clerk as 'he treats Maria as one of his own children'. This was in direct contradiction of Miss Lees' observation of him as recently as July when she considered that he impressed as a man who would not be very accepting of another man's children. No doubt had the case been a contested one that point would have been picked up and the matter probed in cross-examination. Miss Lees was in a very difficult position before the Court because of the multiplicity of roles she was obliged to play, as to which we comment later. That of advocate was not officially amongst them, but one assumes that any conscientious social worker would not allow a piece of evidence to go unchallenged by an applicant in Mrs Kepple's position if she disagreed with it. This was clearly an important question and answer especially as little was said about Mr Kepple in Court and he was not present. Miss Lees however, told us that she did not think the evidence meant any more than whether Mr Kepple was accepting the same responsibility for Maria as for his own children, which was of course a much narrower question. If she misinterpreted the matter in that way she cannot be blamed for not interve ng. This would be a difficult task in any event, which prompts us to indicate our view that in a difficult case such as this one, even if the application is not contested, legal representation on both sides is helpful. It is not for us to consider the much wider and more radical proposition of independent representation for the child.

Maria Colwell Inquiry 1974

The most confusing parts of care proceedings are almost certainly the provisions for the representation of the various parties. Nevertheless, the implications of these provisions are of the greatest importance in understanding the roles which the lawyers involved are playing at various points and for giving appropriate advice to families who become the subject of legal action. It is, perhaps, a mark of the complexity of this area that a whole chapter is needed to discuss what should be fairly straightforward matters.

The Local Authority

The first party in care proceedings is the local authority, as applicants. They will usually be represented by a salaried solicitor from the legal department, although a few places still use specialist officers from social services or even contract the work to private practitioners. Both of these latter options are becoming rare. Occasionally, a barrister may be instructed, especially if the case is particularly complex or a barrister is opposing the application. This is most common in larger cities and in appeals before the Crown Court. If a barrister is to appear, he will be briefed by the local authority's solicitor about the evidence which is to be presented. This evidence will have been put together by the social services' courts staff or, and this is increasingly common, by the solicitor himself. (Women solicitors are not often met in local government.) The representational task is quite straightforward. A view of the child's welfare has been taken by the social services department and it is for the lawyer to lay this out before the court. Such problems as do arise stem mainly from the turnover of lawyers, which is likely to mean periodic re-instruction of particular individuals in the salience of specific technical points. Given the comparative frequency with which a local government lawyer is involved in care proceedings, however, the necessary appreciation of the law and what will constitute key evidence is picked up fairly quickly.

The Child

The other party in care proceedings is the child, following the delinquency model we have already described. This has some rather odd consequences, especially in the case of abused or neglected children where the local authority is, in effect, bringing the action to secure the child's rights rather than to accuse him or her of wrongdoing. The position is rather more straightforward with quasi-offences like truancy or being beyond control, where older children are faced with a fairly clear-cut allegation. As we have observed, these hearings are more like a traditional adversarial confrontation on the criminal model and the child's representative has the clear objective of trying to defeat the allegations or, failing that, to mitigate the apparent severity of the disposition. It is much less obvious that such an objective is necessarily going to be in the child's interest where the allegations centre on parental conduct, whether in terms of abuse or neglect. This section, then, concentrates on those latter circumstances.

What is most likely to happen is that the child's parents, whether on their own initiative or social work advice, will have approached a private practice solicitor when the place of safety order was taken or, at least, when they received formal notice that the authority intended to initiate proceedings. If the lawyer they approach is experienced in these cases, he will know that he can obtain legal aid only if he represents the child. He ought to advise the parents of this and warn them that, if he takes the case on legal aid and decides that their interests diverge from the child's, he may cease to represent them. It is then up to the parents to decide whether they will stick with this lawyer, who may not really be acting for them, whether they will retain him privately or instruct another solicitor, again at their own expense to put 'their' case. If, however, the lawyer is inexperienced in these cases, he may learn that legal aid will be restricted to the representation of the child only after he has applied for it. This could present him with the difficulty that the people whom he regarded as his clients (the parents) will have ceased to be his clients. Does he proceed as if this was a mere 'technicality', or advise the parents to seek legal representation elsewhere at that late stage? This could be hard for him to do if he has acquired any sense of commitment to their perspective on the case.

The task of the child's advocate is fraught with difficulty. If he does keep the parents on, while not promising to represent their views, how much should he tell them of what he discovers about the local authority's case? Above all, how does he obtain sufficient information to make an adequate assessment of the child's case? Does he rely solely on what the parents tell him? Most of the relevant information will, however, be held by the social services department or by witnesses the local authority proposes to call. Does he attempt to make his own 'commonsense' evaluation of the condition of the child? Should he visit the child and try to get to know him? Does he carry out investigations with neighbours? Does he try to attend a case conference? It seems quite clear that his presence would not be considered welcome by most people who arrange case conferences, yet he could argue that, as the child's lawyer, he is indeed one of the most essential members of the conference.

Perhaps the most difficult problem is in the child's solicitor's relationship with the social services department. There is no particular reason why the department should allow its staff to be interviewed or its records to be examined, especially where the result may be to give advance indications of the line it will take in court, enabling the respondent to prepare a more technically effective reply. If the department's staff believe they are acting in the child's interests, then they have a natural stake in making full use of the traditions of adversarial proceedings. It is quite understandable that they should be suspicious of outsiders who also purport to represent the child's interest but who may use the department's own data against it. This is obviously of particular importance given the difficulty which many solicitors have in disentangling themselves from parental instructions as to their children's interests and, indeed, the rather common stance of 'testing' the local authority's case in the examination of witnesses, regardless of the solicitor's private views. Social service records may contain a great deal of confidential material which they would be very reluctant to see come out in court for fear of damaging other parties or, indeed, the prospect of future work with a family and the possible return of a child. It is not possible for courts to order the disclosure of social work files in care proceedings, but where, in other hearings, the point has been pressed by lawyers, the courts have shown themselves very reluctant to assist what are popularly called 'fishing expeditions'.

As far as social services are concerned, these matters are probably best left in the first instance to the authority's legal department. They are, after all, the people who will actually have to present the case in court. If he has been adequately briefed, the authority's solicitor should be clear about the boundary between disclosable and non-disclosable material and is best placed to judge how far his presentation will be compromised by indicating the general lines of his argument. The solicitors are also likely to be personally acquainted, so that the authority's staff can judge their counterparts' sophistication in these proceedings and the degree to which they can be trusted to make responsible use of any information which is shared. In theory, free access is generally likely to act to the authority's advantage. Since proceedings are almost invariably taken only after a serious incident or as a last resort after the failure of voluntary intervention, the case should be hard to shake. A child's representative examining the evidence dispassionately is likely to be persuaded of the merits of the authority's application. This is, however, a rather idealized state of affairs and it is best to follow the guidance of the authority's lawyers, who are aware of the possible hazards of free access to apparently innocuous documents, even at the cost of creating an impression that the social services have something to hide.

We mentioned earlier the notion of the child's solicitor 'testing' the local authority's case in court. At the hearing, the child's solicitor may appear to be adopting a very critical, even hostile, attitude, to the degree perhaps of seeming to 'side' with the parents. Many witnesses find this rather puzzling. Local authority witnesses should not, however, allow themselves to be disturbed by this. Most solicitors who act for children will, at the very least, interpret their duty as being to make sure, by their questioning, that the local authority's case really does stand on a firm foundation. This much, at least, is owed to both the child and his family. There is an element of public policy here. It could be said to be in the public interest generally that the exercise by local authorities of these very wide powers to intervene in family life is open to some rigorous scrutiny in courts, and that it should be able to withstand such scrutiny.

However, the borderline between asking questions to 'test' the authority's case and appearing to oppose it is a very difficult one to draw, and it is unlikely that many solicitors do this in a satisfactory way. Perhaps it cannot be satisfactorily drawn by anyone. The solicitor might take refuge in trying to suggest a middle way between the local authorities' objectives and the interests of the parents, usually by asking the court to make a supervision order rather than the care order sought by the authority (see pp. 90–1). We have argued that here the authority's witnesses must be careful to maintain their view that only a care order will give them the power they think necessary adequately to protect the children.

These problems are compounded by the rarity of such cases for private practice solicitors. Even within a large firm, parents are likely to be sent either to the criminal advocacy section or to the divorce section, neither of which has any significant expertise in child protection cases. As with local authorities, these cases tend to be allocated to relatively junior solicitors as rather low-level work. Thus the solicitor on the case is likely only to be faced with the issues we have posed as he or she goes along. They are not matters on which there is any previously thought-out approach. The solicitor's attempts to master the legal and moral issues involved are perhaps the most common cause of delay in coming to a full hearing of the case.

Having sketched this discouraging general background, it should be said that there are important exceptions. What may seem to some to be a surprising number of relatively experienced solicitors with interests in family matters are aware of the deficiencies of the present system and regard these matters as cases which fall within the broad scope of the social obligations of their firms. This may, on occasion, even extend to free or much-subsidized representation of parents. In some major cities, neighbourhood law centres have developed considerable expertise in this area, although their distribution is very uneven.

It is probably true to say that in many parts of the country parents and children need not want for adequate representation: the problem is to ensure that they end up with the right solicitor. Some social services departments do give parents a short printed list of firms with some experience or interest in child care work. There are certain obvious dangers in this, and parents may feel that they are being offered 'tame' lawyers. Elsewhere, magistrates' courts have also adopted this practice, which may be a more desirable approach, even if the list is actually distributed through the social services. Finally, some magistrates' courts or local authorities will themselves appoint a private solicitor to represent the child. The latter has fairly obvious disadvantages as regards ensuring that justice shall be seen to be done, but the former seems worthy of wider adoption. On the other hand it does have a complication which we explain below.

The Parents

We have already touched upon the parents' problems at various points, and we propose to do no more than bring them together here. Given the delinquency model, parents are not parties to the proceedings. This will not usually matter very much in quasi-offence hearings. Both parents and children may be assumed to have a similar interest in challenging the allegations or avoiding seeming custodial dispositions. It does become rather important, though, in protection hearings, where much of the evidence may relate to the parents' conduct and there is not the same coincidence of interest.

What differences does their not being parties make? Far and away the most important is the unavailability of legal aid. If parents want a solicitor whom they can rely upon to represent their case, then they must either find the money themselves or else locate someone who is prepared to act without charge. The expense is likely to vary depending upon the complexity of the case, the number of hearings, and the area. (Practice costs are, of course, influenced by local wage rates, office rentals and the like.) At 1981 prices, an average case was likely to cost between one and two hundred pounds. Any appeal will probably double this. Such an outlay is likely to be beyond the means of most parents in these cases.

As we have seen, people who are not parties to the hearing have a restricted role within it, but the court has what is known as an 'inherent jurisdiction' to determine its own procedure. Although statutes and rules specify some things which must be done and others which must not, there is a large area of discretion. This means that, for instance, although parents have no formal right to cross-examine witnesses for the local authority or the child, in practice courts are likely to permit this and the parties' lawyers are unlikely to object. The absence of a clear legal right is not allowed to obstruct what the participants would, on commonsense grounds, feel to be fair. The effectiveness of this participation is, of course, attenuated by the problems of getting a lawyer. Commonly, parents are reduced to acting on their own behalf without the benefit of the sophisticated courtroom technique of an advocate. Responses to these circumstances vary, but some help is usually given. The child's solicitor, the court clerk or the chairman of the magistrates may all help the parents to formulate questions for witnesses or put questions on the parents' behalf. Once again, this is not always very satisfactory, but courts are anxious not to leave parents with the impression that they have not had a fair chance to put their side of the case.

There is a further twist which we mentioned earlier. If the child's parents do not choose to consult a solicitor, then they may represent him or her themselves (Magistrates Courts (Children and Young Persons) Rules 1970, rule 17). Once again, what might seem to be a procedural quirk is explicable if one recalls the original drafting of the 1969 Act in its attention to delinquents. Just as an adult who has committed an offence has the right to present his or her own case, so too do juveniles. In recognition of the social view of parents as people who may properly speak on behalf of their children, juveniles may be spoken for by their parents or guardians. This has patently absurd implications in protection cases. On the other hand, the practice, which we have mentioned, in some areas, of appointing a solicitor for the child, and thereby restricting the parents' exercise of this right, has an uncertain basis in law. If the court makes the appointment, it can only rely on the vague concept of 'inherent jurisdiction' as a justification. Once an interim care order has been made, the local authority probably does acquire a statutory power to appoint a solicitor for the child, since it has acquired the full powers and duties of a parent for the duration of the order. Neither of these appointment methods – whether by the court or the local authority – seems entirely satisfactory, since the representation has been arranged either without a statutory basis or by displacing the parents. Both have an obvious potential for creating in the minds of parents a feeling of having been oppressively treated. If and when section 32A of the 1969 Act, a clause introduced by the Children Act 1975, ever comes into effect, the situation will be clarified. As drafted, the clause permits courts to deny parents the right to act on behalf of their children where there is an apparent conflict of interests. Although these provisions are not yet in operation, their very existence has been important in debates surrounding the 1969 Act and we shall, therefore, outline them in the next, concluding, section of this chapter.

Guardians ad litem

The Children Act 1975 made a number of amendments to the 1969 Act which were intended to ease some of the problems we have discussed. With one very limited exception, these have not been implemented, largely for financial reasons.

The central provision is that the Act allows a juvenile court, if it considers that the case may involve a conflict of interests between the child and its parents, to make an order that the child's parents should not represent the child in the case. Since they seldom do anyway, this would not bring about much change were it not for the following provisions which state that if the court does make such an order, it (1) *may* grant the parents legal aid to participate in the case and (2) *must*, unless it is satisfied that this would not be necessary to safeguard the child's interests, appoint a guardian ad litem for the child. If a parent does participate in the court under this provision he may do more than the rules presently entitle him to do, which is only to meet allegations. He will be allowed to 'make representations' as well. However, this distinction is, as we have seen, of little practical importance.

It will be noticed that this system can be brought into operation only if the court perceives a conflict of interests between the child and the parents. It is not clear how this is to be perceived by the court (which, in practice, may mean its clerk) at the early stage when the application is made, but perhaps we can anticipate that courts will assume that there is such a conflict in the normal child protection case. If this happens, it is likely that the parents will be legally represented. The lawyer for the parents will not be under the same contradictory pressures as the child's lawyer presently is, and could be expected to adopt a far more partisan approach in his attitude to the local authority's evidence. This, we would suggest, may be no bad thing, because it will normally be true that the essence of the authority's case is directed against the parents' competence or character. It is only fair that they should be given full scope for defending themselves.

The guardian ad litem will usually be a probation officer, a social worker from a different local authority or a retired social worker whose name is on a panel drawn up for this purpose. It is thought that such a person will be better equipped to assess the child's interest than his or her solicitor, as under the present system. The guardian will be under a duty to investigate the basis of the case, to interview such people and inspect such documents as seem relevant. Having assessed the case, the guardian may either instruct a solicitor or appear personally on behalf of the child. The guardian may make other reports to the court and has a right to appeal on behalf of the child to a higher court against the magistrates' findings. It seems to be anticipated that, in practice, a guardian would always be appointed, except where a child was old enough to instruct a solicitor and could, in effect, determine and speak for his or her own interests.

It is worth noting that although the guardian is under a duty to investigate, the local authority is not under a corresponding duty to cooperate. Given this, many of the problems we have discussed in relation to inquiries by the child's solicitor seem likely to remain. Why should an authority which believes that *it* is acting on behalf of a child assist another party to the possible detriment of its own case and the abrogation of its own duty? This seems to be implicitly recognized in the DHSS circular explaining the provisions, which talks of guardians having a status and experience sufficient to give the social workers in the applicant authority confidence in their judgement. How far the authority's lawyers will feel extensive cooperation to be desirable remains to be seen, if these provisions are indeed implemented.

There is *one* circumstance where these new provisions already apply. This is where the child's parents have applied for the discharge of a care order with respect to their child *and the local authority does not oppose the application.* Since, by definition, these are cases where there is no dispute between the parents and the authority, and most are reasonably straightforward (perhaps confirming an arrangement where a child has been home on trial for a considerable time), it may seem curious that this is the only situation in which these provisions apply. It is made all the more curious by the fact that the court must, in such proceedings, treat the parents as not representing the child, and hence appoint a guardian ad litem, unless satisfied that this is unnecessary to safeguard the child's interest. In all other cases, the court *may* appoint a guardian, unless satisfied that it is unnecessary, but is not obliged to do so. The reasons for the more forceful wording of the provisions relating to the discharge of a care order go back to the notorious case of Maria Colwell in

1974. Maria was returned home after such an unopposed application, against her own wishes and, indeed, those of her foster-parents. Shortly after returning home, Maria was killed by her stepfather. This new provision was brought into effect in order to cover such cases. Whether it actually would do so is uncertain. As we saw, the provision only operates if the court perceives that there is or may be a conflict of interest between child and parents. In the absence of any independent investigative machinery for the courts to probe the local authority's decision not to oppose the discharge application, it is not clear that such a conflict could have been identified in Maria's case. If the courts do follow the general drift of these provisions, however, and assume more or less automatically that a conflict exists, then the time and expense of a guardian's report will be incurred in hundreds of routine cases where this cost is least needed.

It should be apparent that the financial implications of implementing section 32A are substantial: separate representation of parents and children would effectively double the legal aid costs, to say nothing of the guardian ad litem's expenses. Although these constraints are obviously important in the present economic climate, more principled objections have also emerged, many of which relate to our general argument about seeing care proceedings, on a protection basis, as applications to enforce children's rights. If the local authority are not acting on behalf of children, what are they doing? Rather than a three-handed hearing, would it not be better to see these proceedings as an adversarial contest between parents and local authority, where the authority is appearing for the child to ask the parents to demonstrate that they have not mismanaged the trust placed in them? We make this point because many critics of the present system assume that it would be vastly improved by the introduction of section 32A in full. The very existence of the section seems to act as a permanent criticism of the inadequacies of the present arrangement, which is seized upon by those who are reluctant to recognize any role for state intervention on behalf of children. We take the view that, apart from the cost, it is merely likely to aggravate the anomalies, confusions and complexities

of care proceedings. A fundamental re-examination of the
statute is called for rather than ad hoc responses based on
particular cases.

Something of the likely effects can already be seen in
London, and one or two other metropolitan areas, where neighbourhood law centres or specialist practices have become involved with care proceedings. This often means three barristers
in court, and it is increasingly common for further social work
opinions to be sought, especially by the child's legal representatives. These social workers are recruited on an informal basis,
although their costs are payable on legal aid. Their opinion is
obviously likely to be valuable to the child's lawyers in determining their approach, but they lack the special status of a
guardian ad litem. Any evidence given will come through the
witness box and lack the degree of respect which would normally attach to the results of a guardian ad litem's inquiries. The
local authority is probably under even less of an implicit obligation to facilitate their task than would be the case with a duly
appointed guardian. As can be imagined, however, the prolifer-
ation of lawyers and social work assessments complicates the
proceedings and tends to lead to a more formal and legalistic
approach. The deficiencies in procedure, which courts generally
operate in a flexible, commonsense spirit, are inevitably accentuated as technical points are raised. This has led to a good deal
of dissatisfaction with care proceedings, especially in London,
and a greater use of wardship by local authorities. The advantages or otherwise of that course have already been discussed.

This chapter has summarized the provisions relating to the
representation of various interests in care proceedings. Those
relating to the local authority, as applicant, are relatively straightforward. For children, as respondents, and parents, as persons
affected but not party to the proceedings, the provisions are
more complex. Private practice solicitors have great difficulty in
disentangling their duty towards the child, as party, from the
prevailing social attitudes about the special right of parents to
define their children's interests. This problem carries through
into aspects of court procedure, as we showed in discussing the

provisions, not yet in force, for magistrates to order the separate representation of children by appointing guardians ad litem.

Chapter 8

Giving Evidence

We know that social workers often feel inhibited by the hearsay rule of evidence about expressing their opinions in Court. However, it does seem appropriate that, as in this case, an experienced social worker should give expert evidence in the technical meaning of that term.

Wayne Brewer Inquiry   1977

While representation and its implications are perhaps the most technically difficult part of care proceedings, it is the giving of evidence which probably causes more anxiety than any other single element of the process. This chapter focuses both on the nature of the experience itself and on the admissibility or otherwise of what is said. Many people have an image of court hearings which is drawn largely from television or films. The giving of evidence is a dramatic process with the witness as the hapless victim of wily, unscrupulous or hectoring lawyers. Part of this image involves the detailed attention to procedural tricks which narrowly circumscribe what may be said and by whom. The reality of an English magistrates' court is much more mundane. Provided that a witness has clearly thought out what he or she wants to say and has an adequate basis in fact to support this, there is little to worry about.

Becoming a Witness

Anybody who works in the field of health and social welfare may find themselves in court as a witness. This involvement will usually follow from their statements at a case conference or to members of the social services department who are working up a case to go to the authority's lawyers. If called upon to do so, local authority employees must give evidence as part of their conditions of employment. An employee who refuses will almost certainly be exposed to disciplinary action. The same compulsion does not apply to former employees or contractors, like foster-parents, or to employees or contractors of other agencies, most particularly the health services. If somebody refuses to become a voluntary witness, however, the court does have the power to issue a summons, popularly but erroneously called a subpoena, requiring them to attend and give evidence.

Most doctors are prepared to volunteer evidence but health visitors, on the advice of their union, prefer to be served with a witness summons. This allows them to emphasize to families their independence from the local authority and the fact that their evidence is being given under the court's compulsion. General practitioners could also find this to be a helpful procedure, although we would express some scepticism about whether many families really understand the difference. Failure to respond to a summons is contempt of court and a grave matter. Anybody committing such an offence can expect a substantial fine, and the court even has power to order their imprisonment.

The power to compel witnesses is not, of course, confined to the local authority. It may certainly be used by the child's representative and, perhaps, by the parents. This can occasionally be a source of some embarrassment for agency staff who find themselves summonsed to appear, in effect, against their service's case. People like foster-parents, in particular, may find their position rather awkward, since local authorities are often reluctant to jeopardize their goodwill by asking them to appear, and they may find their first indication in a summons through the letterbox. This is very often not something they have bargained for as an outcome of a desire to offer some voluntary service to the community in fostering. What is important to remember is that this is a *court* order. The justices are responding to information given to them about someone who is believed to have evidence which will help them determine the case but who will not come forth voluntarily. The order directs the witness to attend and give evidence *to* the court rather than *for* a party.

The Rules of Evidence

It has been said that the rules of evidence are no more than common sense written carefully. Nevertheless, many people, especially social workers, express great concern about the way their evidence is treated. They often feel that the issues they are dealing with are too vague to satisfy the strictness of legal tests. There is some truth in this at the level of attitudes: lawyers do sometimes give social workers an impression of dissatisfaction with evidence that seems to be based too much on feelings and intuitions and too little on facts. Certainly, lawyers are also inclined to discount social work evidence in favour of medical evidence, especially, but not exclusively, in cases of abuse or neglect. Doctors are considered to make much more impressive witnesses.

There are good reasons for this. Medicine and law have a long-established relationship with fairly well developed conventions and ground rules. Social work is a much more recently created occupation whose tasks and approaches are poorly understood. At the crudest, few lawyers will ever be social work clients while most will be doctors' patients. Moreover, medicine and law have certain conceptual similarities in that they both tend to adopt a rather positivist view of the world. Both are inclined to act as if truth were simply a matter of grasping the right set of external facts. Social work has been much more influenced by relativist philosophical currents which tend to see both 'truth' and 'facts' as rather problematic, not to be seized once and for all as a basis for dogmatic statements.

Social work and legal judgments, then, are rather different. Fieldworkers build up their picture of a family from a variety of sources. This picture is continually subject to revision and re-assessment. The credibility of the basic data can be tested against the worker's personal experience of the family, its kin and its neighbourhood. If necessary, the data can be systematically checked. A court of law cannot do this: reality is assessed at one time for all, like a snapshot. It thus becomes of utmost importance to develop rules, built up over years of experience, which guide courts as to exactly how much credibility should be given to evidence coming from different sources. The court does not have the fieldworker's advantage of instinctive feeling for differentiating the value of various sources. It must act solely on what is said before it in the courtroom. In that context, some forms of evidence will inevitably be considered better than others. The law of evidence is primarily concerned with apportioning the weight which is to be given to such evidence.

What is important is to recognize that these rules do not include or exclude any particular subject matter. They are about procedures for determining truth, for practical purposes, rather than specifying what is to count as truth. As such, they bear a very close relationship to what ought to be good practice in social work observation and record-keeping. This is one of the great virtues of a close association between legal and social service departments in local government. The lawyers can learn more about the evidential basis of social work judgements, while the social workers can see how their practice must be translated, rather than altered, to become intelligible to a lawyer.

Facts, Hearsay and Opinions

Ideally, decisions in court should be made on the basis of factual evidence given by witnesses from their own observation or participation in the events under review. In the nature of things, this is not always possible, of course. The law, then, recognizes other categories of evidence, of which the two most important in care proceedings are hearsay and opinion. Hearsay is where a witness relates what someone else said about X as evidence of the truth of X: for example, where a social worker recounts a neighbour's telling her that he had seen a child being hit as evidence that the child had been hit. Opinion is where a witness draws his or her own conclusions from facts about which evidence may or may not be directly given: for example, where a health visitor infers from fluctuations on a child's weight chart that a child is being underfed while at home. Courts are cautious about hearsay evidence because the person whose statements are related cannot be cross-examined on them. They are also wary of statements of opinion, partly because the facts upon which the opinion is based may be equally as shielded from cross-examination as hearsay evidence and partly because it can be said to be the role of the court, rather than of witnesses, to draw conclusions from facts.

But, while experience has taught the law to be cautious about those categories of evidence, they are not totally excluded. Over the years, a set of rules has been developed which specify the conditions under which such evidence may be admitted and the precautions which must be taken in its use. These rules were substantially liberalized by the Civil Evidence Act 1968, which gave the courts considerable discretion. Unfortunately, this Act has never been extended to civil proceedings in magistrates' courts, such as care proceedings. However, court clerks and magistrates have tended to adopt the more flexible spirit of that legislation, and it is rare to find relevant evidence being ruled out on technicalities. Once again, though, much depends upon local custom and practice, and what follows is our attempt to depict a typical approach, from which departures may be encountered.

Wherever possible, witnesses should try to give direct evidence. This may cover such matters as the behaviour of a child, the state of the home, the conduct of parents towards each other or whatever. It is not good enough to speak in generalities. For instance, if asked about a parent's demeanour in an office interview about financial assistance, a social worker might say: 'Mr Brown was aggressive.' From the court's point of view, this is opinion, although it may well be sufficient as a practical basis for casework. If, however, the social worker were to say: 'Mr Brown knocked my telephone onto the floor, called me a tight-fisted bastard and threatened to punch me in the face if I showed up at his house again. From this, I concluded that he was in an aggressive mood,' the court is presented with facts and an inference, which the justices can check for themselves. To give another example, a health visitor might say: 'Johnny Brown was being inappropriately fed.' It would carry much more force if he or she were to say: 'I made a point of calling at lunchtime on five occasions in that six-week period. On one occasion, I saw this eight-month-old baby sharing a packet of chips with his sister. Once I saw him with a bottle of milky tea. I did not see him fed on the other occasions and could see no baby food anywhere in the kitchen. I thought this was inappropriate for a child of his age.' In both of these examples, the evidence already exists in the workers' observations and reasoned inferences, both of which should, as a matter of good practice, have been fully recorded. What has to be done is to show the court that reasoning, giving both the facts and the conclusions. The court can test the inferences and decide whether the conclusion is more probable than not to be correct.

This direct evidence is much more satisfactory than relying on the hearsay reports of neighbours or relatives. In fieldwork, of course, these may well be rather important, especially as the fieldworker can check the informant's credibility in a variety of ways. If the case looks like coming to court, though, the fieldworker should always try to verify the reports by direct observation. If these reports are crucial to the case, they should be passed to the authority's lawyer with a view to calling their originator as a witness. In making his decision on this, the solicitor will want to know what sort of impression the person is likely to make in the witness box. Will he or she prove reliable under cross-examination? Is the witness vulnerable to accusations of malice, dishonesty, or even inadequate parenting of his or her own children? Any of these could damage the weight of their evidence and have a bad effect on the authority's case.

There is one important exception to the generally cautious view which is taken of hearsay. This is the Humberside Rule, so called from the Divisional Court's judgment in *Humberside County Council* v. *DPR* (1977). Where the person making the original statement is someone who has been looking after the child, whether as a parent, a cohabitee or a living-in caretaker, and the statement is against the interests of the person making it, the statement may be admitted as evidence. The reason for this is that, in ordinary civil cases, people in such a position would be parties to the case. A witness can be allowed to report the statement because its originator is in court and can, if desired, deny it. While parents or caretakers are not technically parties, they will normally be present and may give evidence. So it would be quite in order, therefore, for a fieldworker to report to the court that, for example, the child's mother told her that she had hit the child or that a cohabitee had admitted to coming home drunk. Since these are not criminal proceedings, there is no need to warn people that their statements may be used against them in court, and although a fieldworker may find the task distasteful, it may be advisable in some cases to keep a careful record of what is said by people who have been looking after the child concerning their own behaviour towards the child.

There are some other refinements to the hearsay rule which may not always be appreciated in juvenile court proceedings. Statements of third parties may always be admitted if their relevance is not to prove the truth of what they assert, but the mere fact that they were asserted. It would be proper to report that someone said: 'I am Napoleon,' not as evidence that he was, but because it says something of his state of mind at the time. Similarly, a fieldworker could report that, for example, a wife complained of her husband's conduct, not as proof of the truth of those allegations, but as evidence of the state of the marital relationship.

Occasions may well arise where a statement by an absent party may seem very relevant but would technically fall foul of the hearsay rule. Some of these are settled largely as a matter of common sense. Formally, if photographs or X-rays are produced in evidence, the photographer or radiographer should be called to identify them. The technical point is very unlikely to be taken, and magistrates will probably consider any objection to be time-wasting. More important, perhaps, are verbal statements by parties who cannot now be traced. An example might be reports from an ambulance officer or hospital receptionist to the duty medical officer on their immediate observations of a child's condition or a parent's demeanour. The Civil Evidence Act 1968 contains a procedure for admitting such statements, with certain safeguards, but, again, there is no equivalent in care proceedings. The likelihood is, however, that, since the witnesses (unlike neighbours or relatives) would seem to have no axe to grind, the technical objection would be overlooked, if the evidence is so important.

Agency records are more of a problem. A witness may, and often should, refer to his or her own notes of the case in order to refresh his or her memory while giving evidence. It is not necessary for these notes to have been made at the very same time as the events described, but they must have been written as soon as reasonably practicable afterwards. What this means is that medical notes, which are made during consultations, will almost certainly be admissible. Health visitor records are usually written up when the fieldworker returns to her base at the end of a day's visiting or before setting out the following morning. It is unlikely that their admissibility could be successfully challenged. Social work records, though, are more problematic. It seems to be a rather common practice among social workers to leave these for some days or even weeks, and occasionally to run two or three contacts together into a single entry. Such data are quite useless from a legal point of view and we, personally, doubt whether this really constitutes good practice. We think that a factual account of each client contact should be recorded within twenty-four hours, even if interpretative elements are added subsequently after a chance for reflection and analysis.

All agencies have the problem of past records. The turnover of fieldworkers is often such that a case is being managed by staff who are relatively new to it and themselves dependent on past entries. Unfortunately, these constitute technical hearsay, unless their original authors can be produced. Once more, the Civil Evidence Act 1968 allows such records to be used, with appropriate safeguards, but does not apply in magistrates' courts. This could be a serious problem, especially in cases of

neglect where the authority's case may depend on the accumu-
lated effect of child-rearing practices going back over a considerable period. Fortunately, evidence on the child's current
condition is usually fairly conclusive, and the courts again tend
to be flexible about the admission of these histories. Nevertheless, this uncertainty does not help the authority's solicitor,
although he would be greatly assisted if social workers routinely
and systematically recorded their own observations and relevant
statements made to them so that effective use could be made of
the opportunities presented by the present rules.

Turning to the question of the admissibility of opinion evidence, we should note that here again, as in the case of the
hearsay rule, the law does not seek totally to exclude such
evidence. Both in strict law and in practice it is recognized that
the dividing line between questions of 'fact' and of 'opinion' is
not always easy to draw. The statement 'the car was being
driven fast' is partly a statement of fact but also partly an
inference from those facts as to their cause and their normality.
Similarly, statements like 'the child showed signs of disturb-
ance' or 'the child looked undernourished' combine both factual observation and evaluative comment. So long as there is an
underlying basis of fact for such observations, no court will take
objection to them, although the witness can be expected to
specify in more detail, if asked, the factual basis for the
observation.

There is, however, a degree beyond which such evaluations
pass from what one may call 'commonsense' interpretations to
rely upon a more global assessment by the witness. For example,
general statements like 'the child is in need of psychiatric help'
or 'this parent's behaviour is likely to cause lasting physical or
emotional damage to the child' draw heavily upon the witness's
theories about child development and predictions about future
behaviour. In principle, such statements should only be allowed
if made by people considered competent to make them, so-
called 'expert witnesses'. There is a good deal of misapprehension among fieldworkers, and some lawyers, about what the
legal position in relation to experts really is. It seems, for
example, to be thought sometimes that there are precise rules

designating which categories of professional person are or are not to be considered 'experts'. This is not so. In principle, a court can decide on a witness's expertise in each individual instance. In doing this it may make a pragmatic assessment of his or her qualifications and experience. Sometimes a court will be more impressed by a lay person with many years practical experience working with children than by a newly qualified fieldworker. Whether one agrees with this or not, what should be appreciated is that there is no mystique in the rules about experts: the courts, especially the juvenile courts, respond to witnesses in much the same way as any lay person would.

What is probably more important, even, than the attitude of the court is that of the lawyers, especially those of the local authority. The lawyer is essentially operating on the same lay, commonsense basis as the magistrates, and his primary concern will be to try to present to them the most convincing case he can. Most lawyers familiar with child care cases will be prepared to present a fieldworker to the court as an 'expert' if they think that the fieldworker will impress the court. Not unnaturally they will tend to have more confidence in the more senior workers, and one cannot rule out the relevance of appearance and demeanour. But, given satisfaction on these matters, many lawyers will be prepared to ask fieldworkers questions of general opinion, prefacing the question with a statement such as 'What in your professional opinion would be . . . ?' or 'As an experienced and expert worker in the area of child care, what would be . . . ?' But fieldworkers should always be prepared to back up any opinions they give with factual evidence as far as they can. Any expert is open to questioning in this way. Nothing could create a worse impression on a court than an 'expert' who has been exposed in cross-examination as having based his or her opinion on insufficient examination of the facts of the case.

The necessity of being able to support opinion with fact is particularly important for fieldworkers in the social services departments. By their very nature, their judgements are peculiarly liable to attack under cross-examination by an opposing solicitor or barrister. The reason is twofold. In the first place, there is inevitably a greater degree of uncertainty about such social judgements than there is about more obviously scientific matters. Whether a parent's child care practices are of a totally unacceptable standard or whether a parent's behaviour in relation to the child is likely to improve are less easy to prove than the state of the child's body. Secondly, the evidence of the child's physical condition will much more rarely be the point at dispute in the case. For these reasons, it is true that the evidence of medical witnesses causes much fewer problems in care proceedings. Much of it will be factual, and these facts are unlikely to be disputed. Lawyers will readily admit that they like detailed factual medical evidence, not only of the more obvious kind where a child is physically injured, but also such as is provided by weight charts and developmental tests. In fact, some of this type of evidence is less obviously 'scientific' than it looks, as it makes certain assumptions about the normality of child development which just may not apply in the case of this particular child. Hence the desirability of obtaining such evidence on the child in contrasting settings, especially so that its development in its home environment can be compared with its progress in another setting.

The most important type of 'opinion evidence' usually given by medical witnesses relates to their assessment of the causes of the child's condition. The law recognizes the distinction between this type of evidence and more straightforward evidence of the child's physical state because under section 26 of the 1969 Act a certificate of a registered medical practitioner as to a person's physical or mental condition can be admitted in evidence even if the practitioner does not attend the hearing. But this applies only to factual matters. If the practitioner wishes to make assertions about their cause, then he must attend the hearing and be prepared to be cross-examined.

Presenting Evidence

The preceding sections have described the principles which help to determine what evidence the courts will and will not accept. Before concluding, however, we should like to note some points which can help to maximize the impact of the evidence as it is presented.

When a witness arrives at the court building, he or she will be asked to wait outside the courtroom where the case is being held. It is not usual for witnesses and parties to have separate waiting areas, and this can occasionally be a source of embarrassment. If possible, witnesses should avoid any discussion of the case with other parties or their solicitors. Once the hearing begins, witnesses will be asked to come in one at a time by the usher, who is usually recognizable by a black academic-type gown. The usher takes the witness to the witness box, which in a modern court is generally more like a lectern, and administers the oath. If the witness wants to make an affirmation or take a non-Christian oath, it is as well to speak to the usher before the hearing.

Courtrooms vary a great deal in age and layout, especially when juvenile courts are sitting and there is some attempt to make them more informal. Typically, the three magistrates will sit at one end of the room, possibly on a slightly raised dais. In juvenile cases, at least one magistrate will always be a woman. The court clerk sits in front of the magistrates. The witness stand is usually to the left, as one faces the magistrates, and the dock to the right. In care proceedings, this should be empty, since they are not of a criminal nature. The lawyers may sit either side facing into the middle of the court or at desks across the court facing the magistrates. There will probably be press seats behind the witness stand, although these are likely to be empty, since reporting on juvenile cases is restricted. Finally, across the court and facing the magistrates are seats for the public. The general public are not admitted to juvenile proceedings. Only people with a legitimate interest – other staff from the agencies involved, students or trainees, researchers – are allowed to attend, by permission of the court. Occasionally, uniformed police officers may be present on routine court duties. If they are not actually involved in the case and there is no serious prospect of disorder the court may reasonably be asked to request them to leave.

After being sworn, the witnesses will be taken through their evidence by the lawyer who has asked for them to attend. (We will assume for the moment that this is the authority's solicitor.) Evidence has to be given by means of question and answer. If there are questions a witness particularly wants to be asked, the lawyer should be briefed beforehand. The main point to remember is that an experienced witness tries to give as full an answer as possible during the examination-in-chief. This is the occasion to make the case, and short or monosyllabic answers are useless. Magistrates often find visual aids helpful. Photographs, diagrams, weight charts and the like can all summarize technical points and save time on detailed description. When answering questions, remember that it is the magistrates who are the audience. The solicitor is eliciting a story for their benefit. This means that it is important to speak clearly and slowly enough for them to take notes, somewhere between dictation speed and conversation.

One of the features by which magistrates do assess people is their general demeanour. They recognize, of course, that many witnesses are nervous, but it helps greatly to try to sound confident in what one is saying. It is no good expecting the magistrates to believe evidence if the witness sounds unsure or hesitant. On the topic of demeanour, it is also worth making some effort which shows an acknowledgement of the formal nature of the occasion. Witnesses do not need to dress up as if for a wedding or a funeral. On the other hand, casual dress is, implicitly, likely to be taken as indicating a lack of seriousness and to take away from the status of the witness as someone worth listening to. This may be a cause for regret or irritation, but it seems unavoidable.

After the examination-in-chief comes the cross-examination. This is the point at which the other lawyers for the child or the parents have a chance to test the strength of the evidence. There are a number of techniques, but probably the most common are direct questions, trying to elicit information which has not previously come out, or questions which, in effect, propose alternative interpretations of agreed facts. It is here that the importance of having confidence in one's evidence becomes apparent. What the lawyer is looking for are signs of uncertainty or ambivalence, and his questions are likely to be designed to draw these out. He may ask a question which is phrased to obtain a simple answer when the evidence is more complex. Thus, 'Are you saying that these parents are fundamentally inadequate?' invites a 'Yes' or 'No' answer. Either may lead into difficulty; the former because the lawyer can then go on and point to positive features; the latter because it edges away from the authority's case. Another problem that is often encountered is where the cross-examination asserts that the parents are really willing to cooperate. It can be hard for a witness to reject such offers without seeming harsh and unfeeling. The key advice, really, is to get any reservations in first. If a question can be minimally answered 'Yes' or 'No', the lawyer is entitled to cut in and ask the next question once the answer has been given, even if the witness tries to go on. Rather than answering 'Yes, but . . .', the witness should aim for 'But . . . yes.'

A frequent difficulty is the cross-examining lawyer's lack of familiarity with the structure of health and welfare agencies. Health service personnel, in particular, may find themselves being asked about a child's future in care. They cannot properly answer such questions, which are entirely within the discretion of social services. It is not always easy to refuse, but the best course is for the witness to explain that this is not something they can answer on and to look to the magistrates or the clerk for directions.

One thing witnesses should not be scared of is an aggressive or hectoring lawyer. Magistrates tend not to like that sort of conduct, especially when applied to inexperienced witnesses. Quiet firmness and persistence are the hallmarks of a good advocate. The same, incidentally, is true for the local authority's lawyer. Social workers, and staff from other agencies, are sometimes disappointed by the apparently low-key nature of his cross-examination, but this often bears much greater dividends than an aggressive attack on, say, a nervous mother, which reduces her to tears and forfeits the magistrates' sympathy for the authority. Occasionally, the magistrates may themselves ask questions, as may the clerk. Sometimes, the clerk will, in effect, cross-examine on behalf of the parents if they are not legally represented, or at least help them to phrase admissible questions. Clerks vary somewhat in the enthusiasm with which they adopt this unaccustomed role, and some certainly accord themselves more latitude to attack witnesses than they would allow to any advocate before them.

After cross-examination, the authority's lawyers may re-examine to clarify any ambiguities which have emerged. This is usually very brief, and the witness can then step down. Witnesses may remain in the court for the rest of the hearing, and must certainly not leave the building without the magistrates' permission. The reason for this is that a witness may be recalled at any point, if new material arises in subsequent evidence and the court wishes to reconsider what has previously been said. In practice, this is extremely rare and the courts are reluctant to detain people unnecessarily. If a witness does not want to remain to the bitter end, it is best to mention it to the relevant lawyer, who will then request the witness's release after the examinations have been completed.

It is hoped that this account of the approach of juvenile courts to questions of evidence in care proceedings will go some way in clarifying to fieldworkers the reasons why the evidence of a case as collected and perceived by them is treated in a special way for the purposes of court proceedings. It is also hoped that they will feel less reticence than they sometimes do in considering the suitability of their evidence for presentation in court. It is often thought, especially in cases of emotional neglect, that the kind of evidence available to the fieldworkers would be inappropriate in court, either because of its lack of 'scientific' character or because of the fieldworker's lack of 'expert' status. Field-workers should not be deterred from taking appropriate action for these reasons. It is certainly true that they should be careful to record their observations in the manner suggested above, and be prepared to put their judgements on as substantial a basis as possible. Careful attention to detail will frequently enable this to be done. It is for the lawyer to attend the task of, as it were, 'translating' this evidence into its legally acceptable form in court. Given a sound case which has convinced thoughtful and experienced fieldworkers of the need for court action to protect a child, provided that the grounds fall within the scope of the 1969 Act, there should rarely be any strong reason why a case should not be assembled which from the evidential point of view could respectably be presented to the juvenile court.

Anyone who is involved with child protection work may be called upon at some time to give evidence in care proceedings. If they are not prepared to do so voluntarily, the court may issue a witness summons requiring them to attend a hearing and respond to relevant questions. There are several different kinds of evidence, of which the most important in these cases are fact, hearsay and opinion. Each of these is given a particular weight in the court's deliberations. Witnesses should aim to present their evidence to the court in a coherent and comprehensive fashion.

Chapter 9

Dispositions, Appeals and Further Proceedings

> If the end cannot be achieved by the use of persuasion or personal authority, the existing law provides the means to set a specific requirement which if not met can result in the removal of the child.
>
> *Malcolm Page Inquiry   1981*

It is not our purpose in this book to discuss in detail the legal status of a child who is actually in care. On the other hand, one cannot altogether disregard these consequences in considering whether care proceedings, or other legal actions, are appropriate in a particular case. Moreover, a number of different types of court hearing may follow from care proceedings, and it is as well to give some indication of the issues which may arise. In this conclusion, then, we shall begin by considering the various disposal options which are available to the court and then go on to consider appeals and hearings for the variation or discharge of orders.

Disposition

We have already explained that, formally, the issue of disposition (what order, if any, to make) is separated from that of finding the primary grounds. The main reason for making the distinction is the principle that the court should have access to a wider range of information when deciding what response to make than is necessary or relevant to the first stage. The theory derives from the criminal law (betraying, once again, the original concern of these proceedings with child offenders), where matters such as an accused person's criminal record would be revealed to the court only after he had been convicted for fear of creating unfair prejudice against him. It is by no means clear that any principle whatever supports the two-stage division in child protection cases, although it may be helpful in dealing with quasi-offences.

Nevertheless, the result of the division (if it is followed) is that, after the court makes its first finding, a social inquiry report (or home surroundings report) is usually submitted to the Bench by the authority. The principles upon which this report is drawn up are the same as in cases of juvenile offenders, and social workers will usually be given guidance about its compilation by their department. Reports, in fact, follow a fairly standard form and often cover much of the ground over which the hearing has already ranged. They should give a detailed picture of the family structure and the quality of its internal relationships, as observed by the caseworker. The family's economic and material conditions will be described and then the circumstances in which the family became involved with the social services department, the history of that involvement and the chronology of events leading to the initial apprehension of the child and, finally, to the care proceedings. The report will explain the department's prognosis for the future and their plans for the child. This will lead, finally, to a suggestion about the nature of the order which the authority is asking the court to make.

The report will be read silently by the magistrates, and copies given to the parents through their lawyer (if they have one) and to the child's lawyer. The magistrates (or the clerk) will usually ask the parents if they have any comments to make on the report or whether they wish to query any matters in it with the social worker. This will normally be the first time the parents will have seen the report. Sometimes even the child's lawyer will not have been allowed to see it earlier by the authority. It is very difficult for them to assimilate it in the short time available, and any questions they put will almost inevitably be desultory or irrelevant. In view of the significance of the kind of order made, for both parents and child, this position is not very satisfactory, especially as the contents of the report are not subject to any of the constraints under which evidence is presented in the first stage of the hearing. On the other hand, it is likely to have taken some weeks or even months to get this far, and a further adjournment for disposition, with all the associated distress of another hearing, does not necessarily seem to be in anyone's interests.

The knowledge that parents will have an opportunity to see the social inquiry report should, however, act as some sort of restraint on the compiler. We think that it would constitute good practice to ensure that the report follows the principles we have already set out in our discussion of evidence: general allegations should be substantiated by specific examples, hearsay carefully checked and, so far as possible, interpretation distinguished from fact.

The disposition options have already been described briefly in relation to decision-making before the hearing. We do, however, want to elaborate somewhat on the distinction between care and supervision orders, the most common disposals. Supervision orders are described in sections 11 to 19 of the 1969 Act, and care orders come under sections 20 to 24.

A care order commits a child into the care of a local authority for an indefinite period, terminating on the child's eighteenth birthday, except where the child is over sixteen when the order is made, in which case the order terminates on the child's nineteenth birthday. The local authority is placed under a duty to receive the child into its care and keep him or her there so long as the order is in force, 'notwithstanding any claim by his parent or guardian' (Child Care Act 1980, s. 10). Care orders transfer to the authority all the powers and duties of the child's parents, although the latter are required to contribute to his or her maintenance. The authority's discretion is limited only by a requirement to continue the child's upbringing in the same religion and by the absence of a power to arrange for his or her adoption. Indeed, the authority acquires the right to restrict the child's liberty to the extent that it considers appropriate, without further recourse to the courts. This power reflects the concern with offenders in the 1969 Act. It may, however, be thought inappropriate for children who come into care for their own protection. Obviously, the authority should exercise the control of a concerned parent over the movements or whereabouts of children in its care. On the other hand, where a child in care is alleged to have committed an offence, he or she can be transferred to a secure institution without the protection of a court hearing where those allegations must be properly proven.

The essence of a care order is that the child's future is placed in the hands of the local authority. Parents need only be consulted about the authority's plans for the child or given access for visits and other contact to the degree that the authority thinks fit. Unless there is clear evidence of serious irregularity by the authority, its decisions about a child cannot be challenged in court, except by applications for the complete discharge of the order. The courts have persistently refused to entertain parental complaints about authorities' use of their discretion. Local authorities do not have to institutionalize children on care orders, although they almost invariably do in criminal cases. With protection cases, however, a care order allows an authority to set its own terms for handling a child, a power which may be of great significance where a child's return home can be surrounded by detailed conditions, breach of which can lead to the child's immediate removal. Parents, in effect, become subcontractors to the local authority for their child's care, and retain this status only so long as they satisfy the authority with their conduct.

A supervision order, as we saw, falls considerably short of this. These orders were designed to deal with juvenile offenders. That is why a supervisor is required to 'advise, assist and befriend' the child. Supervision orders normally last for three years. An order may require the child to reside with a named individual if that person agrees, and the supervisor may impose directions about such residence. The order may also include a requirement that the child submit to treatment for a 'mental condition' and be medically examined in accordance with arrangements made by the supervisor. These provisions are seldom used in protection cases because it is normally futile to impose such directions on the young children who are the usual subjects of these cases. It is the adult, not the child, who needs to be directed, or even 'advised, assisted and befriended'. Supervision orders give the authority no further control over the family than it had prior to the hearing, although they may be important in ensuring that a case remains on the social services' active list and that a social worker continues to be involved. A supervision order does not confer on the supervisor any right of entry into the child's home, nor the right to remove the child where this is thought necessary, although the authority may return to the court and ask for the order to be converted into a care order without having again to prove the primary grounds. They may also, of course, use the case in which the supervision order was originally made as the basis of a later application respecting another child, based on the 'same household' ground.

Appeals

Apart from a little-used right of appeal by either party (local authority or child) to the Divisional Court of the High Court in London on questions of law, which are unlikely to be of concern to fieldworkers, the only right of appeal from care proceedings is that of the child. If the local authority loses its case, or if it does not acquire the order it seeks, it has no right of appeal. Once again, the original preoccupation of the system with juvenile offenders makes itself felt, for it is a general principle of the criminal law that the prosecution cannot appeal if the accused person is acquitted. The criminal basis of this legislation is underlined by the fact that the court to which the child may appeal is the Crown Court, dealing with serious criminal cases, rather than the County Court with its extensive jurisdiction in civil and family matters. The absurdity of the system when applied to cases of child abuse or neglect is further accentuated by the fact that this right of appeal is that of the child, not the parents. It is surely ludicrous to confine the only right of appeal from care proceedings to the person for whose protection the original order has been made and to exclude any avenue of appeal for the local authority, which intervened originally on behalf of the child, and the parents, who may have been deprived of a fundamental right as citizens (to bring up their child).

In practice, however, as in other respects, the system has been modified so as to accommodate people's basic notions of justice. Parents were effectively given the right to appeal on behalf of a child by the interpretation of relevant clauses in the 1969 Act in a case, *B* v. *Gloucestershire County Council* (1980), before the Divisional Court. They could, it was held, lodge a notice of appeal in the child's name. A recent decision of the Teesside Crown Court, *F* v. *Durham County Council* (1981), does, however, restrict this right somewhat. In that case, the juvenile court had itself appointed a solicitor for the child, as we described in chapter 7. Having heard the evidence presented to the court from the local authority and the parents, the solicitor formed the view that a care order should be made. He offered no opposition and, once the order was granted, saw no cause for appeal. The parents tried to use the *B* v. *Gloucestershire County Council* ruling to initiate an appeal, but the judge decided that, where the child was independently represented, such action could only be taken by the child's solicitor. It is important to recognize that the Divisional Court's decision is binding on all Crown Courts, whereas the Teesside ruling can only set a precedent in that area. Nevertheless, the case has been widely reported and is likely to influence other Crown Courts. Even where parents do succeed in getting a decision reviewed, of course, they will still have to bear the legal costs themselves. As at the original hearing, legal aid will only be available for the child.

The Crown Court is presided over by a Circuit Judge, and when he hears the appeal from the juvenile court he will be accompanied by two magistrates. The procedure will follow the same form as that in the juvenile court, and the same rules apply as far as evidence is concerned. However, it may well be found that the judge exerts a good deal more control over the proceedings than the magistrates or their clerk did. Furthermore, all parties (and we include the parents for this purpose) may be represented by barristers. It is impossible to give a generalized description of the way the appeal will be handled, because so much will depend on the style adopted by the presiding judge. It is probable, however, that all the matters raised before the magistrates will arise again, and the judge may even allow additional issues to be raised. Sometimes the appeal hearing is thought to be less formal than that before the magistrates, if only because of the greater personal discretion that the judge seems to exercise, but sometimes it will seem more formal, largely because of the (usually) more forbidding setting of the Crown Court.

Further Proceedings

Two other types of proceeding are relevant: applications for variation and applications for discharge.

Variations arise under section 15 of the 1969 Act, where a supervision order is in force but failing to operate through lack of cooperation on the child's part. The supervising authority may apply to the court for the insertion of additional conditions in the supervision order, or for its discharge and replacement by a care order. In these proceedings it is unnecessary to re-establish the original grounds, although the authority's solicitor will normally remind the magistrates of the circumstances. The hearing focuses, instead, on the care or control test and the adequacy of the original order in relation to those needs. Evidence will normally be confined to the supervisor and the child. It should be apparent that even this possibility merely compounds the inadequacies of supervision orders in protection cases. Where supervision fails for lack of parental cooperation, which is plainly important if the subject of the order is a small child, there is no straightforward legal remedy. As so often, of course, much depends on the custom and practice of the local courts and their readiness to disregard such technical points. It is, however, probably better to anticipate and avoid the problem by pressing for a care order in the first instance, even if the authority does not intend to remove the child immediately or permanently.

Although, while it lasts, the care order confers on the local authority the wider powers described above to deal with the child and its family, it is a cardinal feature of committal to care (as distinct, for example, from adoption) that an application may be made at any time to a juvenile court for the discharge of the order. True to the original 'criminal' model of the system, a right to apply for discharge is conferred on the child, not the parents, although the parents are explicitly given the right to make the application on his or her behalf. If the parents seek legal aid, the same problems will arise as those described in connection with the original care proceedings: the certificate will be made out in the name of the child, who, technically, is after all the person who makes the application. It is easy to imagine the difficulties which may arise if the child's solicitor thinks that the child should really stay in care. What he will probably do, however, is formally make the application and present what will essentially be the parents' arguments, although perhaps in a more muted form than they would, so that at least the parents will have the satisfaction of seeing the matters brought before a court once again.

Unlike the case of appeals, however, the right to apply for discharge is not *confined* to the child. The local authority, too, has this right, and indeed this power is essential if the authority has determined that no further purpose is served by keeping the child in its care. In this type of case the hearing is very much a formality, as it is when the parents make the application and the local authority agrees with it. As we have seen, the very ease with which such discharges may be granted was subject to criticism in the light of the Maria Colwell case. The Children Act 1975 introduced a provision, which we described in chapter 7, requiring courts to appoint a guardian ad litem in such cases, where they adjudged that a conflict of interest could exist between a child and its parents. The same Act also brought in another intended safeguard against inappropriate discharge.

Should the magistrates decide that a child remained in need of care or control, even though the original grounds for making a care order no longer existed, they must be satisfied, 'whether through the making of a supervision order or otherwise', that the child would receive such care or control before discharging the order. What this probably amounts to is that the authority must be able to produce convincing reasons to persuade the court that the child will be safe on its return, and if doubts remain, the court will probably want some continuing monitoring of the situation after the child is returned. It will probably feel obliged to make a supervision order (if the original order was a care order) to satisfy itself about this, although as we have already noted, the supervision order in itself gives the authority no greater powers than it would have if it relied simply on voluntary monitoring. But at least the court will feel that it has placed a positive duty on the authority to carry out a monitoring process.

One danger about the present provisions is that there is theoretically no limit upon the number of applications for discharge that may be made. If an application is dismissed, it cannot be resubmitted within a period of three months unless the court gives its specific consent, but this limitation is not very effective to prevent a determined parent from constantly harassing the local authority by repeated applications. Perhaps the only way to deal with this situation is for the local authority to apply to the High Court for the child to be made a ward of court. As we have seen the powers of the High Court with respect to its wards are very wide: they certainly include the power to make an order forbidding the parents to make such applications without first obtaining the consent of the High Court. This order is enforceable by imprisonment for contempt of court if it is disobeyed.

The magistrates' decisions on disposition in care proceedings follow the presentation of a social inquiry report, which gives a general picture of the family circumstances of the child who is before the court. Only two dispositions are in common use: care orders and supervision orders. The former transfer the rights

and duties of parents to the local authority, while the latter
merely require the authority to 'advise, assist and befriend' a
child. Parents, children or the local authority may apply for an
order's discharge or variation, in appropriate circumstances,
but appeals may only be made in the name of the child.

Epilogue

It cannot be pretended that the law relating to child protection is in a very satisfactory state, and much of it has been justly criticized in recent years. The reader of this book can be forgiven for supposing much of it to be unnecessarily complex, and consequently to depend rather more than is really desirable on the magistrates' sense of fairness and their use of discretion. We think that some of this complexity is necessary. What we have at the moment is an intricate set of checks and balances between child protection agencies which constitute an effective safeguard against arbitrary state intervention. However administratively appealing, we would be opposed to much rationalization of the agency system. The divisions of responsibility ensure that action can only follow from discussions between people with independent access to the family and different bases of professional judgement. A consensus must be formed before intervention can occur. We might, however, suggest that the central responsibilities of the local authority and the district health authority, and the imperative necessity of coordination, be underlined by making them jointly responsible for initiating proceedings.

We also have a good deal of sympathy for the place of local discretion, especially in child protection. There are very finely balanced arguments as to how far national standards can or should be applied in this area. In our view, local flexibility, what we might call commonsense justice, has the inestimable benefit of ensuring that the actions of local authorities are subject to local checks in the interests of local popular legitimacy. This may be an imperfect process, but we tend to the view that national government should confine itself to giving procedural guidance rather than trying to determine central standards for child care without regard for local sensibilities.

The major deficiencies, in our opinion, stem from the confusion of delinquent or quasi-delinquent children and young persons with those in need of care or protection. This confusion rests on an unproven identification of the two populations and a misplaced desire to destigmatize juvenile criminals by merging them into a welfare-oriented system. We suspect that the net effect has been to restigmatize children in care through no fault of their own and to bring back the shadow of the Poor Law over those children for whom the state must act as a guardian of last resort. For the delinquent child, serious inroads have been made into many of the procedural protections enjoyed by adults.

In our view, the situation will be improved only when a government grasps the nettle of separating child protection and child delinquency into distinct statutory frameworks, and to some degree reflecting this in the related institutional provision. We have argued that care proceedings are best thought of as a way of calling parents to account for their stewardship of their children. Children are not the personal property of adults: they are future citizens in whose care the whole community has a proper interest. Parents are the trustees for this interest and, like any trustee who fails in their duties, may be replaced by due legal process. We think that child protection issues should be decided, more or less within the existing grounds, by a hearing during which the local authority on behalf of the child asks parents to demonstrate their continuing suitability to act as his or her principal caretakers. In such a proceeding parents would be full parties, with legal aid, and it would be for the court to determine the child's interests between these competing views, in a traditional adversarial fashion.

Within what we might now call 'protection proceedings', we think a new type of disposition would be helpful, to realize the usual intent of a supervision order. Such an order would allow authorities to direct parental conduct, but without conferring a power of removal, other than through the normal place of safety procedures. This might carry a right to enter and inspect the home or to require parents to present their children for day care or medical examination. Children removed from home on protection grounds, and those in voluntary care, should be accommodated in institutions, or other substitute care placements, separate from those who have committed offences. Movement between the two systems should be possible only after a proper legal hearing where a specific offence is proven.

At the time of writing, the DHSS has embarked on a process of consolidating the heterogeneous legal provisions related to children. The first fruits of this are visible in the Child Care and Foster Children Acts 1980. It must, however, disappoint many people – whether professionals, academics, parents or children – that the opportunity for a really thoroughgoing scrutiny of the principles of the child care system has been missed. All we are offered is a scissors-and-paste job by the departmental draftsmen, which may tidy matters up but does little to come to grips with the fundamental issues involved. A Departmental Committee to review the state's responsibilities for the nation's children seems long overdue.

Further Reading

In a book of this nature, we have avoided an extensive use of references or footnotes. Obviously, however, we have drawn on a variety of sources which could be used to follow up specific points.

The first chapter dealt mainly with institutional structures in health and welfare agencies. There are many books which look at these in more detail. Unfortunately the health service will be undergoing a further reorganization before this book is published, and it is difficult to say what impact this will have on local management structures. Probably the most useful source at present is Ruth Levitt's *The Reorganised National Health Service* (third edition, London: Croom Helm, 1980). It is to be hoped that this will receive a further revision in the near future. For social services, we have been helped by Malcolm Payne's *Power, Authority and Responsibility in Social Services* (London: Macmillan, 1979). There is also a useful series of short books, *Studies in the Personal Social Services*, published by Allen and Unwin under the general editorship of Olive Stevenson and Michael Hill. *Child Abuse: Aspects of Interprofession Co-Operation* by Christine Hallet and Olive Stevenson (1980) in this series is valuable in its accounts of case conferences and Area Review Committees.

Voluntary care and wardship are both the subjects of a number of books. The most up-to-date account of voluntary care, based on the Child Care Act 1980, is Alan Holden's *Children in Care* (Leamington Spa: Comyn Books, 1980). For wardship, the definitive account is probably Lowe and White's *Wards of Court* (London: Butterworths, 1979). The best general review of child care law for non-specialists must be Brenda Hoggett's *Parents and Children* (second edition, London: Sweet and Maxwell, 1981). Court procedures and rules of evidence are described in *Child Abuse – Procedure and Evidence in Juvenile Courts* by Jean Graham Hall and Barbara Mitchell (Chichester: Barry Rose, 1978). The lawyers' 'bible' in this area is *Clarke Hall and Morrison on Children* (ninth edition, London: Butterworths, 1977; second cumulative supplement, 1981). For recent court decisions, the best places to look are the case reports in *LAG Bulletin* and *The Journal of Social Welfare Law*, both of which also carry articles on child care law from time to time.

Index

Books of Related Interest

The Practice of Social Work
General Editors: Bill Jordan and Jean Packman

Social work policy is shaped by practice, and is dependent on good practice for its proper implementation. This series is concerned first and foremost with personal, face-to-face processes and problems in social work: issues of policy are introduced through issues of practice. The editors and authors stress the crucial importance of understanding. The reactions of clients to their problems and to the guidance and sympathy offered by social workers are given equal weight to discussion of the appropriate methods and techniques.

The series is not restricted to any particular theoretical stance or practical approach, but draws upon as wide as possible a range of methods of work and social work settings – statutory and voluntary work, field and residential, casework, group, community, generic and specialist work – with every group of clients.

The books in the series are for students of social work and for social workers.

Mate and Stalemate
Janet Mattinson and Ian Sinclair
'An engrossing account. . . . The revealed picture is a fascinating one; and the portraiture of the clients is careful and compassionate.'
New Society

Growing Up in Care
Barbara Kahan
'It is hard to imagine that Barbara Kahan's book will not be invaluable for many years to come to social workers.'
New Society

Creative Social Work
edited by David Brandon and Bill Jordan
'A much-needed reminder of what social work and the social worker is all about.'
Times Educational Supplement

Children, Grief and Social Work
Gill Lonsdale, Peter Elfer and Rod Ballard
'Cannot fail to be of value to all who are contemplating social work with families and children facing deep crises.'
International Journal of Social Psychiatry

Occupational Survival
The Case of the Local Authority Social Worker
Carole Satyamurti
'A remarkably balanced and insightful study of a social services department.'
Times Educational Supplement

Children and Divorce
Martin Wilkinson
'Indispensable for everyone involved in divorce court welfare work.'
Times Higher Education Supplement

A Place Called Hope
Caring for Children in Distress
Tom O'Neill
'An unquestionable must for every parent, teacher, social worker and magistrate.'
Times Educational Supplement

Kids at the Door
A Preventive Project on a Council Estate
Bob Holman
'His simply-told and humble story should be read widely by academics, by students and by field-workers.'
New Society

A Bridge to Independence
The Kent Family Placement Project
Nancy Hazel
'It leaves the reader with a considerable number of uncomfortable questions but also with a strong impression that there has been a breakthrough.'
Adoption and Fostering

Other Related Titles

Receiving Juvenile Justice
Adolescents and State Care and Control
Howard Parker, Maggie Casburn and David Turnbull

'This is a topical, important and controversial book. It is topical because it provides original evidence and discussion to add further fuel to the debate about juvenile justice and welfare. It is important because the evidence it records shows the complexity of the juvenile justice and welfare system, and the difficulties of finding a solution to the justice/welfare dilemma. It is controversial because it suggests that the actions of some policemen and magistrates may not illustrate a concern for justice and the welfare of young people.'
Youth in Society

'Carefully researched and documented, and highlighted by copious direct quotation from the participants in and victims of the system, the whole book is a disquieting illumination of serious inequalities in processing and sentencing in different areas. It destroys the lingering myth of the impartiality of British justice. It is perceptive, compassionate and thought provoking, and is a work which is easy to read and should be widely read.'
New Society

Probation Work
Critical Theory and Socialist Practice
Hilary Walker and Bill Beaumont

'The publication of this book is an important event. Most of the
extended literature on the probation service is either hopelessly
out of date, very dull, or both. This book offers a lively chal-
lenge to everyone in the service.'
Probation Journal

'A fascinating book which takes a realistic and intelligent look at
the functional and technical problems facing the probation
service today. . . . one of the most stimulating books I have
read for a long time.'
Apex News

'Closely argued, well referenced . . . makes a unique contribution to critical thinking not only about probation but also
about social work in general.'
Social Work Today

The Child's Generation
Second Edition
Jean Packman

'A well-written and fascinating account of the birth, life and death of the children's service. . . . essential reading for social workers and health visitors in training.'
Health and Social Service Journal

'This thoughtful study raises many important questions for child care in the future.'
Times Higher Education Supplement

'For those coming to a study of social policy in relation to children for the first time, the book . . . provides a sound and admirable introduction. The reader familiar with the already available literature . . . will certainly gain from the thoughtful and lucid presentation of the material, and from the sense of perspective on current problems.'
British Journal of Social Work

Mental Illness and the Law
Tony Whitehead

This book is a straightforward guide to British legislation concerned with mental health, how it is implemented, and how it can affect people's lives.

The Mental Health (Amendment) Bill introduced during the 1981–82 Parliamentary session has put forward some important proposals for changes in legislation, and has also acted as a focus for public debate on the whole question of mental illness and the law. Dr Whitehead examines its proposals alongside the existing provisions of the 1959 Mental Health Act so as to give an accurate and up-to-date picture of both current legislation and likely reform. He also describes the differences in the laws prevailing in Scotland and in Northern Ireland.

Introductory chapters look at the different kinds of mental illness, treatment and the mental health services, and there is an appendix of forms currently in use in England and Wales. A glossary of psychiatric terms is provided for reference. *Mental Illness and the Law* is a useful handbook both for people confronted by mental illness in family or friends and for doctors, lawyers, magistrates, social workers, the police and other professionals in the field.

Girl Delinquents
Anne Campbell

Why are girls delinquent? Why should they steal, fight and run away from school, family and friends? Is female delinquency substantially different to the male variety? Are social attitudes towards delinquent boys and girls different? Should they be? These are some of the questions to which this book – one of the first in its field – is addressed.

Anne Campbell searches for the causes of female delinquency in family, education and class background and examines adolescent girls' values and the pressures upon them. As well as considering recent work in Europe and the United States, she draws extensively on her own research and includes many excerpts from conversations with teenage girls that vividly convey their own viewpoints and beliefs.

Further details of books of related interest may be found in our Social Work, Social Policy and Sociology catalogues. For free copies, please write to:

Promotion Services Department
Basil Blackwell Publisher
108 Cowley Road
Oxford
OX4 1JF